LIVING WITH AMBIGUITY

LIVING WITH AMBIGUITY

*Religious Naturalism and
the Menace of Evil*

DONALD A. CROSBY

STATE UNIVERSITY OF NEW YORK PRESS

Published by
STATE UNIVERSITY OF NEW YORK PRESS, ALBANY

© 2008 State University of New York

For information, contact State University of New York Press, Albany, NY
www.sunypress.edu

Production and book design, Laurie Searl
Marketing, Anne M. Valentine

Library of Congress Cataloging-in-Publication Data

Crosby, Donald A.
    Living with ambiguity : religious naturalism and the menace of evil / Donald A. Crosby.
        p. cm.
    Includes bibliographical references and index.
    ISBN 978-0-7914-7519-5 (hardcover : alk. paper)
    ISBN 978-0-7914-7520-1 (pbk. : alk. paper)
    1. Nature—Religious aspects.   2. Naturalism—Religious aspects.   3. Philosophical theology.   4. Good and evil.   I. Title.

BL65.N35C76 2008
202'.12—dc22   2007042266

10 9 8 7 6 5 4 3 2 1

for all my students

Through the years you have inspired, challenged, and often confounded me with your written and oral questions, observations, and arguments, giving me the privilege of working with you as your teacher and fellow learner.

CONTENTS

PREFACE

I'm sitting on my back porch enjoying the wonders and beauties of nature. Birds are singing in the trees, squirrels are scampering about, the camellias are in bloom, the sky is a brilliant blue, and the grass is moist and glistening after a recent rain. All seems peaceful and at rest. But in the pond below my back yard a blue heron has just caught a frog in its menacingly sharp beak, and somewhere nearby a red-tailed hawk is eagerly tearing and consuming the flesh of a small bird it has captured and killed. The faint wail of sirens can be heard in the distance. Is there a fire? Has there been an automobile accident? Has someone just suffered a stroke or been shot? Are fire trucks, ambulances, and/or police cruisers speeding to the rescue or, in the case of the police cars, to apprehend a criminal?

While I enjoy the serenity of nature in my back yard, a frog and a small bird have met violent deaths in order that the heron and hawk can have their dinners, and a person or persons have been injured—perhaps severely—or someone is in imminent danger of dying from a clot in his or her bloodstream, or someone will be arrested for a crime.

Here we have the ambiguity of the whole of nature in miniature. Tranquility and suffering are there. Beauty and horror are there. Life and death are there. People living in harmony with one another are there, as well as people committing crimes, some of them grievous and horrible, against one another. The world, both human and nonhuman, is a relentless, inexorable blend of goods and evils.

How can we expect to find solace and strength in such a world, especially if it is itself viewed as the object of religious faith? Is it possible to live an active, fulfilling, and deeply meaningful religious life without a belief in God or a religious faith that centers on God? How and to what extent can such an outlook and way of life cope with the disruptions and threats of evil in the world? How can we live with any amount of confidence and hope in the face of such a world? Answers to these questions are offered in this book, which outlines a version of religious naturalism that focuses entirely on nature and does not incorporate or require any conception of God.

Religious naturalism in general is the view that nature is metaphysically ultimate and that nature or some aspect of nature is religiously ultimate. There is nothing beyond, behind, above, or below nature. Nature requires no explanation beyond itself. It always has existed and always will exist in some shape or form. Its constituents, principles, laws, and relations are the sole reality. This reality takes on new traits and possibilities as it evolves inexorably through time. Human beings are integral parts of nature, and they are natural beings through and through. They, like all living beings, are outcomes of biological evolution. They are embodied beings whose mental or spiritual aspect is not something separate from their bodies but a function of their bodily nature. There is no realm of the supernatural and no supernatural being or beings residing in such a realm.

I describe, develop, and discuss here implications of the version of religious naturalism I term "religion of nature." In an earlier book entitled *A Religion of Nature* I depicted and defended a vision of the metaphysical ultimacy of nature and went on to show how the whole of nature so understood could be regarded as the appropriate focus of resolute religious commitment and thus qualify as religiously ultimate as well. In that book, as well as in this one, I argue that a thoroughly demanding, richly fulfilling, and wholly adequate religious life can center on the complexity, depth, and mystery of the natural world, with no need for appeal to a supernatural world or to beings, presences, or powers supposed to belong to such a world.

The present book is a sequel to the earlier volume. It is primarily concerned with the problem of how religion of nature conceives of and enables us to cope with two fundamental types of evil in the world. The very word *evil* evokes a shudder, the chilling breath of something dark, inexplicable, and deeply threatening. Our structures of meaning are in constant danger of being shaken and shattered by our confrontations with evil in its two primary forms. The first is what I call "systemic natural evils," that is, those destructive forces of nature that are not direct outcomes of human decisions or actions but that may cause extreme suffering for sentient beings—including human beings—and that can devastate regions of the natural environment. Examples are predations, diseases, accidents, floods, storms, earthquakes, and fires. The second type of evil is moral evils, the evils—some of them hideous in their characters and effects—that human beings bring about through their choices and actions (or deliberate inactions and neglects) and inflict upon one another, upon other creatures of nature, or upon aspects of the nonliving environment.

How does religion of nature interpret and understand the sources and characters of these two types of evil? How does its interpretation compare and contrast with the responses to evil in other religious traditions? Most importantly, what resources does religion of nature provide for coping with the menace of these evils in our lives? And how adequate are these resources? These questions are especially pressing and urgent in view of the fact that religion of nature as I conceive it is a form of religious faith without a God or gods; without the idea that the world as whole has an overarching purpose or design; without any supernatural source of revelation, guidance,

forgiveness, or strength; and without hope of an afterlife of everlasting bliss
that is alleged in some religions, particularly the theistic ones, to compensate
humans for the sufferings, sorrows, and injustices of this life.

I do not sentimentalize, minimize, or underestimate the dire threats
of evil in this book. In fact, I include graphic, shocking, sad examples of
both systematic natural evils and moral evils in order to show how utterly
serious is the problem of finding and affirming meaning in the face of evil.
*This is a profound and vexing problem for all religious traditions and for human
life in general.* In my view, the menace of evil is a central, if not *the* central
problem with which all religions must wrestle. This problem goes a long
way toward explaining why there is the need for such a thing as religion
in the first place.

I affirm the religious ultimacy and rightness of nature despite nature's
rampant ambiguities of good and evil. I contend that it is a mistake to confuse
religious goodness with moral goodness. There is, alongside the moral and
aesthetic species of value, a distinctively religious species of value which I
go to some lengths to characterize and defend. Moral values and religious
values have important interrelations which I discuss, but they are not the
same. The religious rightness of nature is for me unequivocal. But nature
exhibits a radical ambiguity of systemic and moral goods and evils. I argue that
this ambiguity is not avoidable. It cannot be eliminated in any conceivable
universe. Nor would we *want* it to be when we properly understand its true
character. The inevitable price of the systemic natural and moral goods of
the world is its systemic natural evils and the potentiality of its moral evils.
Neither can be had without the other or the possibility of the other.

In an extended discussion I invite the reader to try to imagine a world
without these two forms of evil, and I argue that it is not only difficult in
the extreme to imagine what such a world would be like but that, even if
it could be conceived, it is not a world in which we would want to live.
Most of the goods that we now instinctively cherish and take for granted
would be absent in such a world. Ambiguity is built into any robust and
genuinely desirable world, then, and our natural world—despite and even
because of its ambiguities—is worthy of our utmost religious trust, devotion,
and commitment.

The evils remain evils and stubbornly persist as such in this analysis.
They are not swallowed up into a supposed good of the whole or made
negligible or dismissable in comparison with that whole. Their character and
menace as evils is starkly clear. But this book's thesis is that *we need look no
further than nature itself* to find in the splendor, dynamism, and rejuvenating
powers of the natural world—and within ourselves as remarkable creatures
of nature—reliable sources of both sustaining and demanding hope, purpose,
and value for the living of our lives. This can be so even as we acknowledge

and prepare ourselves to confront the deeply threatening and irreducibly real manifestations of evil in the world.

With gratitude I acknowledge my considerable indebtedness to the insightful suggestions, questions, and criticisms communicated to me in writing concerning an early draft of this book by J. Thomas Howe, Tyron L. Inbody, and Jerome A. Stone. Each of these perceptive scholars has stimulated me to think more deeply and I hope more adequately about issues raised and discussed throughout the book. I am also grateful for the support given to the book by two anonymous readers for the State University of New York Press. My wife Pamela Crosby has encouraged and supported me through all the stages of the book's development. She has raised numerous pertinent questions about its arguments and claims and made many helpful suggestions about ways to improve its content. She has also assisted me with the proofreading and preparation of the Index. Her presence in my life is a cherished example of the workings of natural grace I describe herein.

ONE

RELIGION OF NATURE AS A FORM
OF RELIGIOUS NATURALISM

Ah, nature! subtle beyond all human subtlety, enigmatic, profound, life-giver and life destroyer, nourishing mother and assassin, inspirer of all that is best and most beautiful, of all that is most hideous and forbidding!

— W. MacNeile Dixon, *The Human Situation*

We humans are persistent questioners. We like to get to the bottom of things. We are not simply creatures of instinct, responding automatically to circumstances of the natural environment in our urge to survive. Instead, we possess consciousness, reason, and freedom to a degree that no other creatures of earth apparently do. These qualities enable us to stand out from the natural environment in our conscious minds rather than being immersed in it. They confer upon us a capacity and need to reflect upon both the environment and ourselves in a critical, searching, detached fashion. As a result, the more inquiring ones among us tend to speculate intensely about our world, seeking to understand its character, the how and why of its existence, and our proper role as humans within it. We crave intelligibility, purpose, and meaning in our outlooks and lives. We are not satisfied with mere survival. The history of cultures and civilizations is suffused with evidences of this relentless human quest for comprehension and meaning. Down through the ages, in story, myth, and rite, in philosophy, science, and art, the search goes on.

Two major styles and outcomes of this search are religious supernaturalism and religious naturalism. The "religion of nature" of this book's initial chapter title is a particular version of religious naturalism, as we shall presently see. Supernaturalists seek resolution of the most perplexing and pressing questions of existence in a realm above or beyond nature. They

1

are convinced that the natural world points ineluctably beyond itself to a transcendent ground that accounts finally and fully for its origin and continuing existence and that bestows upon it enduring significance and value. The task of human life is, then, to orient oneself, one's society, and all the aspects and enterprises of one's existence around this transcendent ground of meaning and value, and to seek in it definitive answers to life's deepest questionings and yearnings.

In the Western part of the world, the supernaturalist form of this persistent human search has led to belief in the existence of God, conceived as a distinct being who is the source and sustainer of the universe and everything within it. Consider, for example, Thomas Aquinas, the most prominent Roman Catholic theologian of the High Middle Ages. He reasoned that the natural world and everything in it is contingent upon or dependent for its existence upon something wholly other than itself, a single transcendent being that exists necessarily. While things of the world come into being and pass away, that upon which they depend has no beginning or end. This self-sufficient, self-explanatory, eternal, and therefore by definition supernatural being, he observed, "All men speak of as God" (*Summa Theologica* Q. 2, Art. 3, in Aquinas 1948: 26).

According to Aquinas, God commands our utmost reverence and obedience, and he[1] has given compelling evidence of his reality and saving purposes for us and all his creation in our experience and reason, as well as in gracious, more specific revelations of himself in scripture and tradition. This theistic, supernaturalistic answer to the central enigmas of human existence is echoed in the Protestant Christian tradition by the *Westminster Shorter Catechism*, composed by Puritan divines in 1647. "What," queries the *Catechism*, "is the chief end of man?" Its confident answer is, "To glorify God and enjoy him forever." End of question, end of story. Muslim and Jewish thinkers have reasoned similarly.

Aquinas's picture of the universe and its utter dependence on God can be compared to a mobile.[2] A mobile, it will be recalled, is an ornament hanging from roof or ceiling by a cable, rope, or thread. It contains several arms or bars of different lengths, some of which are suspended from the central thread and others from subordinate threads. From these bars hang various kinds of objects. Everything is carefully calibrated and balanced, so that the mobile can gently rotate and sway in the wind. In doing so, it combines the dynamism of its motions with the artful order of its design. Crucial to the mobile's operation is the mounting point for its central thread. Let us suppose that the mobile is the type that can be bought in a store and that is contained in a small box. One unpacks the mobile, assembles it, and searches for a place to mount it. Suppose that one mounts it with a thumbtack in a plasterboard ceiling and steps back to admire its graceful undulations and circlings. All is well, but were the thumbtack to come loose, the mobile would tumble to the floor and lie there in discombobulated ruin.

The case is similar with Aquinas's conception of God. The whole universe hangs suspended from God, as it were. All of its inherent motions and changes, as well as its stability and order, are critically dependent upon him. Were God's support to be taken away even for a moment, the universe would collapse into a meaningless heap. It would be reduced to the kind of primeval chaos, "without form and void," talked about in the book of Genesis prior to the divine creation of the world. More pointedly, it could not exist at all.

Religious naturalism removes the supposed thumbtack from the ceiling. It makes no reference to a supernatural realm or to a God, gods, goddesses, or spirits thought to exist in such a realm. It sees no need for a supernatural ground or support for the world. For it, the world exists through its own immanent principles, resources, and powers. Without God, it does not collapse into ruin. For the religious naturalist, if anything exists necessarily, it is the natural world itself. It gives rise to, sustains, and explains all else that exists. No appeal need be made to anything beyond or above the inexhaustible, self-sufficient splendor and providingness of the world itself. Nature in some shape or form is all there is now, ever has been, or ever shall be. It spawns and supports all its living creatures, including human beings. For the religious naturalist, nature or some aspect of nature is also the ultimate source of value and meaning for human life. It or an aspect of it is therefore the appropriate focus of religious faith and dedication.

Since religious naturalism does not accept the idea of a supernatural realm standing over against nature, it also does not affirm or feel the need for any sort of revelation coming from such a realm. All religious knowledge and awareness are based on endeavors of humans to respond to religious meanings and values implicit in nature itself. Moreover, there is no supernatural source of forgiveness, empowerment, or salvation. These resources must be found in nature itself. Religious naturalists may speak of such things as transcendence, grace, and spirituality, but they regard them as operative entirely within the natural order—an order of which human beings are an inseparable part.

As we would expect in light of their focus on nature, religious naturalists take seriously the methods and findings of the natural sciences. They seek to develop religious outlooks upon and conceptions of nature consistent with those methods and findings. They are especially impressed with the sweeping scientific saga of the evolution of the universe, the earth, and life forms on earth. However, not all religious naturalists place sole reliance upon descriptions and explanations of natural phenomena provided by the natural sciences. Some of them insist upon supplementing these invaluable scientific perspectives on nature with insights and understandings derived from other fields of study such as the social sciences, arts, and humanities, and from the experiences of daily life. They argue that, since humans and their cultures and histories are integral parts of nature and expressions of potentialities of nature, the full range of human experiences needs to be taken into consideration, and from as many angles as possible.

Finally, religious naturalists tend not to give credence to the traditional religious idea of the survival of humans in an afterlife, whether in some kind of heaven or hell or in a sequence of reincarnations. They take this idea to imply a kind of supernaturalism, which as naturalists they reject, and as lacking convincing empirical support. For them, while salvation may continue to be an important and meaningful religious concept, it can have nothing to do with a life beyond death. It relates exclusively but importantly to the quality and contribution of human lives here and now.

I have given the name "religion of nature" to the version of religious naturalism to be argued for in this book, partly to demarcate it from other types of religious naturalism, but also to label its distinction from the various and generally more familiar (at least in the West) supernaturalistic forms of religious faith. In the remainder of this chapter, I first indicate religion of nature's principal themes. Then I describe some chief issues confronting this type of religious naturalism today. Finally, I comment more fully on the last of these issues, which brings into view the radical ambiguity of nature—especially as considered from a moral perspective—and questions on that basis nature's fitness as the proposed focus of religious faith. This issue is the main topic and concern of this book. Subsequent chapters of the book will explore the issue in detail and seek to defend the appropriateness and adequacy of religion of nature as a religious response to the fundamental needs, cares, anxieties, hopes, aspirations, and responsibilities of human beings in the context of a bright and bountiful but also dark and threatening natural world. A significant part of the ominous, fearful character of life in this world is a proneness of human beings and their institutions to deliberate acts of brutality, hate, and destruction, on the one hand, and to callous indifference toward remediable suffering and pain, on the other—a tendency to which so much of human history bears sad and unimpeachable testimony.

PRINCIPAL THEMES OF RELIGION OF NATURE

In a previous book (D. A. Crosby 2002) I presented the outlook of religion of nature and laid out arguments for it as a profoundly inspiring and richly fulfilling religious stance. Some features of this stance will be developed further as the present book unfolds. But in this chapter I want briefly to indicate the principal themes of religion of nature as a type of religious naturalism so that these themes can be borne in mind as we consider and critically assess the adequacy of its approach to the troublesome and often menacing ambiguities of nature—a nature on which it nevertheless rests the whole weight of religious faith.

Religion of nature agrees with the general characteristics of religious naturalism outlined above. It has no recourse to supernaturalism in any of its forms. It finds the whole significance, point, and purpose of life in nature alone. It relies solely upon the resources of experience and reason in arriving at its religious vision. And it does not look beyond nature for religious inspiration, strength, or empowerment. It has deep respect for the natural sciences. It has no concept of continuing life beyond the grave but places all of its emphasis on enhancing the quality of the finite span of life for all natural beings, human and nonhuman, both in the present and on into the future.

For religion of nature, humans are not the crown or apex of nature but simply one of the products of its evolutionary processes. They are integral parts of nature and intimately connected with all other living beings in both time and space. Humans are not entitled to dominate nature but should seek to live in harmony and balance with the rest of nature. Earth is their capacious home, and for that they should be grateful. But they should also accept and act upon the responsibilities implicit in this fact, treating with grace, kindness, and consideration all of their fellow members of this diverse household.

Some more specific traits of religion of nature, however, are the following. In contrast with some forms of religious naturalism, it does not speak of God, gods, goddesses, or animating spirits of any sort, even if these terms are used metaphorically or symbolically, or are viewed as aspects, potencies, or processes of nature. It makes no attempt to align itself with such existing religious traditions as those of Christianity, Judaism, or Islam. Nor does it purport to be a revision of, or a more adequate, more current, or more relevant development of, any of these traditions. Its metaphysics of nature is derived, not merely from the findings of the natural sciences, as important as these are for it, but from other fields of thought and expression as well, and especially from the dynamics of lived experience in all of its forms.

Religion of nature rejects the kind of fact-value distinction that locates all the facts in the so-called objective world, especially as that is depicted by the natural sciences, and all of the values in human subjectivity. Nature, for it, is replete with values and disvalues as well as facts, and the values and disvalues are not confined to the human part of nature. Its concept of nature, moreover, does not rest solely on the evidence of the five senses but assumes the critical relevance of other types of experience as well, for instance, experiences of recollection, anticipation, consummation, continuity, change, emotion, imagination, valuation, judgment, intention, and choice. It contends that an adequate account of nature and its constituent beings must encompass all of these kinds of experience.

Religion of nature strives also to be constantly aware of how much there is about nature and about ourselves as natural beings that we do not know and cannot know. Our perspective as human beings is but one perspective among those of innumerable other living beings on earth, to say nothing of the possibility of conscious beings elsewhere in an incredibly vast universe. It is limited by what our meager five senses can tell us, even when supplemented by instruments; by what we can infer from other aspects of our experience; by what we are able to imagine, conjecture, or surmise at any given time; and by what the capacities and limitations of our linguistic, logical, or mathematical systems permit us to reflect upon and express. For religion of nature, nature is not knowable through and through but is wreathed with clouds of impenetrable mystery. Even its most familiar and well known aspects can become inexhaustibly wondrous and miraculous when analyzed in depth or approached with an innocent eye undistracted by previous habits of thought.

Religion of nature's focus is on the whole of nature and not on some particular aspect of it, despite—and more pointedly because of—the admitted ambiguities of nature viewed in its entirety. Reasons in support of this seemingly counterintuitive statement will be presented later. Religion of nature also argues for a distinctively religious kind of value and resists the idea that there must be a smooth coincidence or consistency of religious and moral values. The two are related in various ways, but they are not the same. Religion of nature's concept of religious rightness or value, therefore, should not be taken to imply or to require the unqualified moral goodness of the object of religion. Such a firm distinction between religious and moral values goes against the grain of much religious thinking in the West today, including that of many professed religious naturalists. It is widely assumed that an essential quality of any religious object, whether it is thought to be God, a particular aspect of nature, or something else, is that it be unambiguously good in the moral sense of good. Taking issue with this assumption will be an important part of our continuing deliberations in this book.

Finally, in common with other religious naturalists and in strong contrast with thinkers such as Aquinas, I think of nature as existing necessarily, not contingently. That is, it is not dependent upon something beyond itself for its existence. It needs no transcendent ground but always has been and always will be, in some shape or form. However, the nature I conceive as existing necessarily is not simply the nature we experience at present but all of the different forms or faces of nature that ever have been or ever shall be. To use the language of Alfred North Whitehead, ours is but one "cosmic epoch" in a succession of such epochs throughout limitless time (Whitehead 1978: 91). Each epoch exhibits its own characteristic principles, laws, and constituents, but no one of them, including our own, exists necessarily. Each comes into being and passes away.

I draw an important distinction in this connection that W. L. Reese traces back at least as early as the Dominican encyclopedist Vicente de Bauvais (c.1190–c.1264) and that was later put to use by such eminent thinkers as

Giordano Bruno and Benedict Spinoza (see Reese 1980: 380, 611–12). The distinction is between nature natured (*natura naturata*) and nature naturing (*natura naturans*). Any given cosmic epoch, with its stable features stretching over eons of time (nature natured), is pervaded and underlain by a restless, unstable, stubbornly innovative process or power (nature naturing) that brought it into being as a radical transformation of a past epoch and that will eventually bring about its own dissolution and replacement with a new epoch, a new kind of nature natured. This succession of one epoch by another throughout endless time is made inevitable by the fact that nature exhibits not just causal continuity and regular causal laws but a relentless, ever-present discontinuity and novelty that will inevitably erode and override its existing structures. Thus, the nature that exists necessarily and throughout all time is nature naturing, something fully natural but not to be identified merely with the character of nature as we presently experience it. At its most fundamental level, nature is process, not pattern. This everlasting process works within the contexts of patterns that come into being and pass away. Nature naturing and nature natured are thus tied inextricably together. Process becomes pattern and pattern yields to process—within the turbulent origins and dominant patterns of our present world and through a trajectory of worlds without end.

The fact that nature is a coalescence and tension of nature natured and nature naturing draws attention to its inherent volatility and dynamism. Its creations and destructions go hand in hand and work unceasingly in all its epochs, including our own. There is a stable context within which these processes of creation and destruction go on, but even this overarching stability is relative and subject to eventual change. While it persists, many kinds of transformation and change are continually taking place, some of them sudden and unexpected. This restless tension, instability, and unpredictability of nature's processes account for its awesome fecundity and amazing evolutionary developments but also for much of its ambiguity.

This kind of ambiguity is rife with seeds of menace and danger to humans and to all living creatures. They can prepare themselves for nature's sometimes abrupt changes and succeed in avoiding harm from these changes in some ways, but not all. From their respective standpoints nature, so warm and welcoming at one time, can present at another time a countenance of horrendous destructiveness and evil. This type of ambiguity in nature is accompanied by other types we will discuss later. Together, the various manifestations of nature's ambiguity comprise a serious and daunting problem for religion of nature and other naturalistic religions—and, if the truth be told, for all types of religion and for all forms and conceptions of human life.

CHIEF ISSUES CONFRONTING RELIGION OF NATURE TODAY

Religion of nature, the religious outlook that lies at the heart of this book, runs counter to much conventional reasoning about the character of religion and how it functions or ought to function. In so doing, it brings to light certain issues or problems that make it difficult in the climate of today's thinking even clearly to comprehend, much less seriously assess, religion of nature's own central claims. Reflection on these issues should help to clarify what these claims are and why religion of nature sees fit to make them. The last issue to be reflected upon is of particular importance for this book as a whole. Here is a list of what I consider to be the chief issues, along with a brief response to each one.

1. There is a deeply etched assumption, particularly in the Western mind, that religion must focus on some kind of personal God or gods, and an accompanying propensity to identify any sort of admitted nontheism with an outright rejection of the meaning, importance, or value of religion itself. Religion without belief in the existence of God or gods is therefore viewed either as a thinly veiled contradiction or as simply too dilute gruel to supply much needed religious nourishment. But in denying the existence of a personal God or gods claimed to exist in a supernatural realm, religion of nature does not thereby reject religion or dismiss the critical importance of religion for human thought and life. It finds profound religious meaning and value in nature itself.

Two examples of impressive and enduringly influential religious outlooks that do not conceive of the religious ultimate as personal are Theravada Buddhism and Advaita Vedanta Hinduism. Religions such as Taoism and Shintoism join forces with religion of nature and other kinds of religious naturalism in centering attention on the immanent powers and mysteries of nature rather than upon some kind of separate, nonnatural domain. And one of the West's most penetrating thinkers, Benedict Spinoza, was an intensely religious man who did not conceive of God in either personal or supernatural terms. In fact, he identified God with nature. So religion of nature's denial of a personal deity or deities and a realm of the supernatural should not deter us from acknowledging its seriousness as a form of religion or its feasibility as a candidate for religious faith. Defense of this seriousness and feasibility will occupy us throughout this book.

2. There is the prevalent notion that the universe as a whole must have some purpose or goal given to it by a creator God in order for there to be significant purposes and goals in human lives. But these two issues are separate, not intimately related as has long been thought. We can and do find many kinds of purposes, values, and sources of meaning in our lives, ones that can be discovered and cherished from within and do not need to be conferred upon us from without. So to deny the existence of God or the divine creation of the world is not to strip the world of purpose. While there is not, for religion of nature, a purpose or intentional design of the world as a whole, there are plenty of purposes to be discovered and acted on within the world. The second kinds of purpose do not require the first kind.

For example, all creatures, including humans, typically yearn to preserve themselves and to live and flourish. It is in their nature to do so, and there is no logical necessity for the yearning to be traced back to God. Whether or not God exists, people find purpose, value, and meaning in such commonplace, everyday things as their vocations, families, friends, deeds of service, love of country, intellectual endeavors, aesthetic experiences, outdoor adventures, hobbies, play, and so on. And religion of nature claims that ultimate fulfillment and value can be found independently of any divinely conferred purpose by learning to live gratefully and responsibly as a natural being.

This can be done by seeking continually to enliven one's awareness of the awesome significance of being an outcome of complex natural processes stretching back into the remote past and a conscious participant in and contributor to those processes; by exploring and learning to appreciate the wondrous intricacies and interdependencies of nature; by discovering how to actualize the gift of one's irreplaceable uniqueness as an individual; by putting this gift to use in serving one's society and working to protect and preserve the natural environment; by being open to transformative possibilities in events occurring beyond one's prediction or control; by being deeply sensitive to the suffering of one's fellow humans and of all the creatures of earth; by contributing as fully and effectively as one can to the alleviation of those sufferings; by finding ways to help increase satisfaction and joy in the world; by humbly acknowledging and accepting the limits of one's own finitude and the modest place of humans within the whole of nature; and by coming to terms with the precarious equipoise and changeableness of all things natural. Here are purpose, challenge, and meaning enough for many lifetimes.

3. In our culture, there is a widespread assumption that salvation means going to heaven when you die and that if there is no such thing as personal survival in an afterlife, this present life can have no meaning. Religion of nature's denial of an afterlife and its locating all religious meaning and value in this life might be regarded, therefore, as grossly inadequate and unfulfilling. A singular virtue of this denial, however, is that it places the emphasis of religious life upon something other than oneself. It is not one's survival after death that is of supreme importance but the contributions one can make before one dies to present and future generations of living beings, both human and nonhuman. Selflessness rather than the everlasting survival of one's particular self is therefore at the crux of religion of nature's conception of the religious life. This conception seems more genuinely altruistic and more likely to avoid the temptation to use one's religion simply as a means to gratify one's personal wishes and desires.

The notion, moreover, that life can have value only if it exists forever flies in the face of everyday experience and common sense. I value my life, and my wife values my life as I value hers, even though neither of us believes that we will live forever. Are we deluded or being illogical? I think not, because it needs to be recognized that the value of a human life is enhanced rather than diminished by awareness of its not being immortal. It can be seen as something inestimably precious, something to be cherished by and for others and lived with special fervor and outgoing dedication by oneself—because it will not be here forever and because the significance of one's life has so much to do with how it is lived, with its relations to others, and with what it contributes to others in the limited span of its years.

4. An assumption closely related to the third one is also common in today's religious thinking. The assumption is that the ideal form of existence is disembodied and independent of the physical world. It amounts to a denial that we are creatures of the earth, that we belong here and can be at home here. Religion of nature's firm emphasis on our embodied existence and on our character as natural beings is opposed to this assumption, and it is susceptible to being dismissed out of hand because of the assumption.

The assumption is strengthened, I believe, by its association with the traditional Western conception of God. God is conceived as pure spirit. God has no body and is not dependent on anything bodily for his existence. This also means that God has no need of the world. He can exist, and once did exist, before the Creation, in complete independence of the world. Humans are said by traditional Western theism to be created in the image of God, which is often thought to mean that they too, in their essential nature, are pure spirits with no essential relation to anything natural or bodily. They can realize their true natures, then, only in a life beyond this world, a life of complete disembodiment and pure spirituality. An afterlife in a purely spiritual realm or form of being is assumed to be absolutely necessary for them to be fully and completely what they essentially are as creatures of God, made in his image.

The mind-body or spirit-nature dualism being assumed here can be called into question in a number of ways. We do not have space to go deeply into them, but four ways of doing so can be briefly mentioned. One is that earlier Jewish, Christian, and Islamic teachings, when they speak of an afterlife, tend to do so in terms of the resurrection of the body, not the survival of a disembodied spirit. They thus envision a greater degree of continuity between this life and the next than do later theologians of these traditions who are by then deeply influenced by the mind-body dualism of Platonic and Neoplatonic thought. The second way of questioning this dualism is recognizing that when God creates the heavens and the earth in the book of Genesis, he pronounces it good. He does not condemn it or reluctantly tolerate it because it is not purely spiritual. The first man and woman are placed in a garden replete with skies, land, trees, fruits, animals, and the like, not in a disembodied realm. And they themselves are embodied, created from the dust of the earth.

Thirdly, if God is totally distinct from the world which he has created, how could he relate to it? If there is nothing in common between himself and his physical creatures, how could he interact with them? This is a theological version of the familiar impasse Platonic and Cartesian dualisms encounter when they try to explain the interrelations of a purely spiritual mind with the wholly different body it is thought to occupy for a limited period of time or with the physical world in which it is believed temporarily to reside. Finally, the full weight of evolutionary and ecological thought in contemporary science favors the idea that we are emergent natural beings, not purely spiritual ones, and that we crucially depend upon the whole of the physical nature of which we are a part. We are embodied beings through and through, therefore, and not disembodied ones. We do not need an afterlife of purely spiritual existence to fulfill our true natures. This is religion of nature's view.

5. There is a deep-rooted tendency in our culture to draw a sharp line of separation between human beings and their cultures and histories, on the one hand, and nature on the other. We tend not to see all features and productions of human life as manifestations of nature but oppose them in our thinking to nature. Thus, we commonly talk about "going out into nature," not recognizing that we are always in nature wherever we are. We are in nature in our homes, on our streets, in our cars, in our offices, in stores, in schools, in libraries, in factories, etc. Or we think of nature exclusively as wilderness or of nonhuman animals as radically different in kind, not merely in degree, from us. We even tend to forget that we ourselves are animals. There is a difference, of course, between human artifacts and the productions of nonhuman nature, for example, rocks, mountains, rivers, and trees. But in creating artifacts we are actualizing potentialities planted in us by nature. We are doing our thing just as the beaver does its thing in chewing down aspen trees and using their trunks and branches to build a dam. We do our sorts of thing with more self-awareness, variety, and imagination than the beaver does; beavers do not compose symphonies or build space ships, for example. And they do not use language or write novels or scientific treatises. But our human cultures and histories in all their creativity, splendor, and complexity are manifestations of our capacities and gifts as natural beings.

When we take these ideas seriously, we realize that we are dependent upon nature for everything we are, have, or are capable of producing or doing. We are integral parts of nature, not beings set over against it or capable for a moment of living outside it. We cannot insulate ourselves from nature or safely ignore our responsibilities to it. In being responsible for it, we are responsible for ourselves. If we fail to live up to our responsibilities to the nonhuman aspects of nature, dire consequences for ourselves, our cultures, and our civilizations can ensue. There are evidences of such threatening consequences all around us in today's world.

Religion of nature does not enjoin us to run out and hug trees, but it does remind us that such things as trees, plants, bogs, algae, and phytoplankton supply the oxygen without which aerobic life—including our own life—would be impossible. The proper contrast, then, is not between nature and culture, because the latter is simply a subset or one kind of expression of the former. The proper contrast is between the human and the nonhuman aspects of nature. And these two are indissolubly linked. This fact shows how deeply immersed human beings and their creations are in the natural order. It is the source and sustainer of their life and capabilities; it bestows upon them all the individual, social, and cultural potentialities made manifest in the course of human history. And if nature is that which exists necessarily, as religion of nature contends, then it is not only metaphysically ultimate. Nature can be brought into the arena as a serious contender for religious ultimacy as well.

6. The final cultural assumption standing in the way of open-minded consideration of the claims of religion of nature is the idea that a fit object of religious faith must be unqualifiedly and unquestionably good in the moral sense of good. There must be no taint of ambiguity about its goodness. It must not only be the source of all things good in human life; it must be the absolute standard for human moral living. We must be able to look up to it as the paragon of moral righteousness and chief exemplar of moral law. For example, if we think, as did St. Anselm of Canterbury (1033?–1109), of the religious ultimate as "that being than which nothing greater can be conceived" (Anselm 1948: 7), then it would seem obvious that we must include in the meaning of the term *greater* the idea that the religious ultimate surpasses all else in its moral greatness or absolute moral goodness. A contemporary philosopher, William L. Power, does not hesitate to draw this conclusion (Power 1997: 135).

The problem with nature being considered as the object of religious devotion, then, is that nature does not exhibit unqualified moral goodness. For one thing, nature is not a conscious moral agent. For another, it has an aspect of restless volatility that can mean destruction as well as creation. And as we have already observed, its creations and destructions go together. It destroys in order to create, and its ensuing creations are subject to its later destructions. As a consequence, nature can sometimes present a face of menacing horror. The rains of its calamities fall upon the just as well as the unjust, the innocent as well as the guilty. Its evolutionary history is rampant with extinctions. It is a system of predations in which one form of life must kill and consume another in order to live. It is suffused with suffering, starvation, and disease. And all its living beings inevitably die. Finally, the history of its human life forms includes unspeakable acts of malice and hate, as well as much studied indifference to the sufferings and pains of humans and other creatures.

How, then, can nature be a fit object of religious faith? If we are to live with religious confidence, must we not place our faith in something above and beyond nature, something unquestionably secure, dependable, and good? What hope of salvation can a radically ambiguous nature ensure? If nature's ambiguity is the ultimate truth and all there is, how can we live in the face of that ambiguity? These are serious concerns, and they pose a fundamental challenge to religion of nature—a challenge that is the central issue to be discussed in this book. I will make a start on responding to this sixth assumption and dealing with the concerns it brings into view in the next section. The concerns will be addressed more fully in the chapters to follow.

QUESTIONING THE SIXTH ASSUMPTION

One of the problems with the sixth assumption is that it posits a radical disconnection between the putative moral purity of the religious ultimate and the moral ambiguities of the world. But if a morally pure religious ultimate has given rise to and/or sustains the world, why should there be such ambiguities? And why should they continue to be tolerated? In the case of traditional monotheism, this is the theological problem of evil: if God is all good and all powerful, he is presumably opposed to all evil and fully capable of eliminating it altogether. Why, then, is there so much evil in the world? Does not the fact of this evil call into grave question the existence of such a God? There are two proposed solutions to this problem that I regard as inadequate. I shall briefly present them and explain why I think them to be deficient. If they are set aside, as I believe they should be, then the idea that a religious ultimate must be unambiguously good in the moral sense of good must continue to be questioned.

The first proposed solution is what has been called the free will defense. Presented by the philosopher John Hick, among others (see Hick 1966, 1990), it argues that the good of human freedom, which enables humans to attain personhood through their own choices and efforts, also necessarily allows for the evil of bad choices. God has created humans with freedom so that they can relate to him as persons, not as automata, but in so doing he risks and allows the misuses of their freedom and their falling into evil. Moreover, in order for them to be truly free, they must live in a world that permits the meaningful exercise of their freedom, with all its consequences. This must be a regular, orderly, predictable world. In such a world, however, they can be hurt. Fire, for example, not only warms; it harms if it is not used carefully. To be free to make use of fire is to be capable of hurting oneself or others with it. If it did not have predictable character and effects, humans could make no use of it. The case is similar with the gravity that mercifully binds us to the surface of the earth. If we stumble off a precipice into thin air, we are likely to be maimed or killed.

Or to cite a more commonplace example, if I can execute my freedom to open a door, the door and its surroundings must have regular, predictable properties that can be affected by my choices.

In this way, the free will defense seeks to explain both moral and natural evils. Genuine freedom presupposes the possibility of evil choices, and to be capable of choice we must live in a predictable world by which, if we are not careful, we can be hurt. Furthermore, we will sometimes get in the way of the world's processes in situations that are not under our control, and these processes can do us harm. The final wrinkle in the free will defense is the idea that God graciously and freely limits his absolute power in order that we can be free and the world can function with some degree of autonomy or independence of his immediate control. In other words, he gives to us and the world slices of his power pie. At any time, however, he can, if he chooses, take back those slices and exercise his power to override human freedom and the autonomy of the world. His absolute power, therefore, is not compromised in any way.

But of course it is compromised to the extent that humans are able, by their bad choices, to thwart his purpose and will for them and other parts of his creation. As human history so clearly shows, that thwarting of moral goodness has taken place on a massive scale and continues to do so today. God is presumed to allow innocent beings, both human and nonhuman, to be hurt, punished, persecuted, and killed by evil doers and evil institutions, with no apparent recompense or recourse. Political persecutions, slavery, rampant economic injustice and exploitation, the firebombing of cities, concentration camps, genocides, humanly caused extinctions of species, and severe environmental despoliations are examples. And God continually allows terrible things to happen to human beings and other creatures of earth which they did not expect and which they had no ability to control: earthquakes, fires, famines, storms, floods, diseases, accidents, and the like. Is this the sort of world God intends? If so, it is a world plagued by ambiguity, an ambiguity that stands in stark contrast with the supposed absolute moral goodness of God. It gives little comfort to be assured that God can prevent these things when he so routinely refuses to do so.

Of course, the proposed answer is that it is all worth the price if the goods of human freedom and personhood are preserved. These goods are assumed to trump and redeem all the moral evils they allow and the natural evils they require. Humans can learn, if not immediately then over long periods of history, how to use their freedom responsibly and how to enter as fully developed persons into fellowship with a personal God. If they do not succeed in learning to do so in this life, then they can in a life to come. This answer might tempt us were it not for the fact of *so much* evil throughout the history of the world, for the fact of *how many* innocents—human and nonhuman—have already suffered and continue to suffer, and for the fact that all the previous failures to use freedom responsibly lie in an *irretrievable* past, along with all the widespread and often excruciating suffering and pain they have produced. Even if there is progress among humans over historical time or in an afterlife toward responsible personhood, the past and its colossal sufferings and evils for humans and nonhumans alike must be seen, by this argument, as mere grist for the grinding of the historical or heavenly mills, an expendable means to the later achievements of human beings. Is the allowance of such expendability, and on such a sweeping scale, completely and unqualifiedly moral?

Do we begin to see the radical ambiguities in this picture and how fundamentally they call into question the existence and role of an assumedly unambiguous, unerringly moral creator and sustainer God? So long as God's supposed absolute power is held in abeyance, he must refrain from interfering with either the autonomy of human freedom or the autonomy of the world. Implicit in these two autonomies are radical ambiguities. God's allowance of them, even if for the sake of the undeniable goods of human freedom and personhood, imparts ambiguity to God's own acts and decisions. He must sacrifice one kind of good for the sake of another. He must allow rampant evils for the sake of important goods.

God's presumed unqualified, indisputable moral goodness is compro-mised or at least made seriously questionable by the stark evils he permits. His intentions may be said to be good, but the effects of his actions are interlaced with evils. A troublesome and often horrendous intermixture of evil with good is the best he can do, if the world is to have autonomy and humans are to be free. All of this adds up to an ironic kind of abso-lute goodness and absolute power. It tells us something about the world in which we live and the character of our lives in this world. Perhaps both kinds of ambiguity, natural and moral, are ineradicable in any imaginable world. It is difficult, at any rate, to conceive a clear relationship between the ambiguities and a morally unambiguous and absolutely powerful God or to understand how the conceptual conundrums they pose can be resolved or eliminated by belief in such a God. The theological problem of evil is not unhorsed; it sits securely in the saddle. An explicit statement of this fact, and therefore of the ineluctable moral ambiguity that attaches to the God of the Bible, is contained in the book of Isaiah. There God proclaims, "I form the light, and create darkness, I make peace, and create evil. I am the Lord, that doeth all these things."[3]

A second way of trying to retain the conception of God's absolute moral perfection in the face of the evils of the world is that of process theology. In this approach, exemplified by the depictions of God's nature and role in Alfred North Whitehead's *Process and Reality* and developed further by theologians and philosophers who think in this vein, God's complete goodness is insisted upon, but his absolute power is denied. God's power is limited, not by his free choice—as in the free will defense—but by necessity, because he has not created the world, and the world has its own immanent principles and powers. In this vision, neither God nor the world is completely autonomous; each depends crucially upon the other. The inherent relative autonomy of the world means that it is not completely under God's control, either in principle or in fact.

God seeks to lure every aspect of the world toward its highest possible attainment in the way of value, but those aspects have the power to resist the divine lure and to go their own way, at least within limits. God's absolute moral goodness is claimed by process theists to be preserved by the character of his lure and by how he responds to what has already happened in the world. He always does the best he can with what the world makes available to him. He lures the world to its highest possible attainments of value, given the possibilities for value presented by the causal past. And he preserves forever in the immediacy of his everlasting experience all the value, however limited in particular cases that might be, that has been achieved in the past. His absolute goodness is unsullied and uncompromised, then, despite the recalcitrance of a world marred by imperfections and evils of its own autonomous doing.

The forfeiting of God's absolute power for the sake of his absolute goodness looks promising, at least from the standpoint of logical consistency. But does it really save God's intentions and actions from the taint of ambiguity? I do not think it can, and for two reasons: the fact that God's perspective is limited by the multiple perspectives of the world's entities, and the fact that the future is not completely predictable and becomes increasingly less so the more remote it is from any present standpoint. No matter how intelligent and wise God is considered to be, his perspective cannot wholly encompass and include all the other perspectives of the world. We will comment more fully on the perspectival character of reality later on, but we can note here that, in Whitehead's metaphysics, the world is made up of a multiplicity of perspectives he calls actual entities and of the perspectives of the larger systems comprised of those entities. Each entity and system is unique in character and occupies a unique standpoint in relation to the rest of the world. As such, its perspective contains some degree, however large or small, of incommensurability with other entities and systems.

This must be as true of God as it is of the things of the world, meaning that God's perspective cannot encompass or capture everything about those things. Each and all perspectives are privileged by virtue of having something in them distinctly their own. Therefore, God cannot know everything there is to know about each of them, much less comprehend them completely and fully all at once. Each perspective has its own claim upon the world, the insistent particularity of its autonomous standpoint and being. Since this statement also applies to God's perspective, his perspective—however perspicuous, comprehensive, or wide-ranging it might be deemed to be—must be acknowledged to be finite not infinite, limited not limitless.

This insistent particularity of perspectives becomes especially notable in the case of sentient beings such as animals and humans. Their autonomous self-expressions and demands upon the world are not completely compatible with one another. In order for the effects of some to be maximized without constraint, those of others would have to minimized. Even seeking carefully to balance these particularities in relation to one another means sacrific-ing some aspects of one or more of them for the sake of aspects of others, assigning to the balance or harmonization of perspectives more value than the intrinsic value of any one perspective. Whitehead claims, of course, that God seeks a balance of perspectives that will keep them from being at cross purposes and allow each of them to have as much individual expression or significant role in a given circumstance as possible. But the point remains that the achievement of such a balance means giving up some potential values for the sake of others. The ambiguity of such a balance is built in. Whether we accept Whitehead's metaphysical account or not, the same problem pertains to any kind of world in which there are a plurality of entities, each with its own individuality and particularity of self-expression. As we shall see in a later chapter, plurality, perspectivity, and ambiguity go necessarily together.

The upshot is that God's perspective is partial and cannot do full justice to all other perspectives, and that in seeking to balance all the perspectives at a given time in relation to one another in order to achieve the maximal goods of such balancings, some potential goods—namely, the attainments of each individual entity or system of entities considered in isolation from all the others—must be sacrificed. Since God's perspective is necessarily partial because he is limited by a perspective unique to himself, God cannot know with absolute certainty what is best for any given entity or set of entities. And since he seeks a harmonization of the possibilities for value in a multiplicity of entities, possibilities bound to conflict with one another in various ways, that harmonization must be bought at the price of sacrificing some potential value or values. Which values should be sacrificed, and why? Given the partiality of the divine perspective, not even God can answer this question with absolute certainty. God's decisions about the matter have to be burdened with some degree of uncertainty. And the sacrificing of some goods for the sake of others, that is, allowing some evil of the privation of some potential goods for the sake of some other goods, is a necessity that not even God can avoid.

The problem is compounded when we consider the uncertainty of the future. In determining his lure for present entities, God has to consider the effects that lure is likely to have, if fully responded to, on the future. And in preserving the achieved goods of the past, God has to make some judg-ment about what the goods are. This judgment must include the effects of putative present goods upon the future. These considerations and judgments are bound to be less certain the farther they are projected into the future. For Whitehead, the future is genuinely open, even for God. This means that his predictions of it can only be probabilistic at best. To put the point another way, God is capable of making mistakes in his moral judgments and other judgments about value, because he cannot be completely certain about the effects of present events on future ones.

Can Whitehead's God avoid being shackled with moral ambiguity, then? It would seem not. God's judgments may be thought to be far wiser and more inclusive than the judgments of any worldly being could be. But it is hard to see how they can be regarded as infallible or completely immune from the kinds of ambiguity that plague human moral judgments or permeate a world of multiple sentient beings, each with its own sorts of at least partially incommensurable needs, desires, deserts, and demands.

An example might help to make this point clear. In the last year of the World War II, the United States had the option of bombing two cities in Japan with a newly invented atomic weapon. By doing so, it was then believed, an end of the war could be achieved swiftly, and hundreds of thousands of lives could be saved. Those lives would include those of the allies forced otherwise to invade Japan and of all of the Japanese who would die trying to defend their soil. The leaders of the United States, Great Britain, and the Soviet Union decided that the loss of lives brought about by the bombing of Hiroshima and Nagasaki, even with the deadly radiation fallout it would produce, could be justified by the saving of countless other lives it would make possible. They sent an ultimatum to the Japanese leaders urging them to surrender or suffer great destruction. The Japanese did not respond to the ultimatum, and the bombs were dropped on their two cities.

But neither the leaders of the allies nor anyone else could be absolutely sure that such a terrible price had to be paid. Perhaps other options would have been better, such as a demonstration of the atomic bomb's fearsome power in an open field away from the congestion of a city, or awaiting the Soviet Union's promised entry into the war in the Pacific, which might have accelerated the peace process. But would either option have brought about a quick Japanese surrender? No one could be sure at the time. Nor could the leaders of the United States weigh with absolute certainty the effects for the future of having their country be the first to use such a weapon in warfare. No matter what position we may take concerning the wisdom or folly of the decision that was made, we cannot deny its ineradicable uncertainty and ambiguity. There is still room for different interpretations of its morality by competent moral judges, showing that its deep moral ambiguity continues to this day.

The question for us, then, is what would God have decided, and why? Could God somehow have avoided being entangled in the ambiguity of the situation and choice? I cannot see how we could exempt him from that ambiguity. At the very least, he would have had to allow for the sacrifice of some enormous goods in order to bring about the achievement of others. And he could not have known the future consequences of any of the available decisions with absolute certainty. This does not mean that God must now be regarded as immoral or unfeeling, but it does mean that it no longer makes sense to think of his decisions as absolutely, unqualifiedly, unambiguously moral or as providing for an unquestionably best moral outcome. The problem of the world's ambiguities remains whether one endorses the free will defense of God's absolute power and goodness or the process conception of God. As we have seen, this problem necessarily involves God as well, infecting his decisions and actions with ambiguity.

So long as God is said to have any relations to the world, including that of creating it in the first place, the problem of moral ambiguity in God remains. If we want to think seriously about a religious ultimate, we must take fully into consideration its relations to the world. Should we fail to do so, the assumed ultimate would cease to have relevance to our lives. Since neither theism nor religion of nature can escape the problem posed for their respective religious ultimates by the moral ambiguities of the world, the sixth cultural assumption, namely, that a fit object of religious faith must be free of all traces of moral ambiguity, is not decisive as an objection against religion of nature. The assumption is open to serious question, given the fact that neither of the two versions of theism we have discussed can satisfy what it requires. In the next chapter we shall probe more deeply into the moral ambiguities of nature, both human and nonhuman, showing in greater detail why these ambiguities are inevitable and ineradicable. In subsequent chapters we shall see why, despite and even because of these ambiguities, nature qualifies as a suitable, splendid, and saving focus of religious faith and commitment.[4]

TWO

AMBIGUITIES OF NATURE

[T]he real world is a world of lice as well as butterflies, horse piss as well
as vintage champagne, and to the person who has truly realized this, one
is as good as the other. To insist otherwise is to make an impious demand
of existence which it is unwilling and unable to satisfy. The "ugly" things
of life exist, and the only question is how we are to confront them.

—Francis H. Cook, "The Jewel Net of India"

One way to characterize the ambiguities of nature is to observe that nature is
a mixture of goods and evils. However, Francis H. Cook, in his paraphrase of
the thought of D. T. Suzuki quoted above (see Suzuki 1971: 237), speaks of
the pernicious, annoying, "ugly" aspects of nature—and he presumably means
to include its most menacing and destructive aspects as well—not only as
"good" but as *equally* good with all its other aspects. My own view, stated in
the first sentence of this paragraph, would seem to be in sharp conflict with
that of Suzuki. I am noting that nature is a pervasive intermingling of goods
and evils, and he is saying that it is entirely good. The apparent conflict
is resolved, however, when we recognize that "good" can be interpreted to
mean quite different things in the two observations. Suzuki is saying that
the whole of nature is good from a *religious* perspective—in his case, from
that of his own Zen Buddhism—and with this affirmation I heartily agree.
Nature for me as well as for Suzuki is *religiously* good.

However, nature is obviously not wholly good in other respects. Consider
the crassly immoral acts committed by some human beings and the effects
of these acts upon the world, or the sufferings and calamities to which all
of nature's living beings are susceptible. As we saw in the previous chapter,
nature should not be conceived as something separate from humans. Our
appraisal of it must therefore give due notice to the evil deeds humans
have committed and continue to commit against one another and other

21

parts of nature. These deeds are not transformed into goods simply because they are acts of a natural being and because nature as a whole is claimed to be religiously good. This would be a facile "whole-part" way of thinking in which the evil of the parts is thought to be swallowed up into and made negligible by the good of the whole. Moral and religious types of goodness do not amount to the same thing.

Similarly, the sufferings, destructions, and disasters nature's processes visit upon humans and nonhumans alike cannot be regarded as good from their perspectives. Such a notion would be hopelessly insensitive and naïve. Living beings can be thrown into a panic by such things. They are in danger of being deprived of food or habitat, separated from kith and kin, subjected to tormenting pain, grievously wounded, or caused to lose their lives. None of these effects are good in every sense of that term, however normal or inevitable a part of nature's processes they may be said to be. Once again, the religious goodness of nature does not trump or eliminate its undeniable evils.

CONCEPT OF RELIGIOUS RIGHTNESS

Moral evils and what I shall term the "systemic natural evils" experienced vividly as such from the standpoints of nature's sentient creatures are aspects of nature that should not be downplayed or trivialized. They should be readily acknowledged as serious types of evil, even if we are still to insist, as I do, upon laying uncompromising emphasis on the religious goodness of nature. In emphasizing the religious goodness of nature, we should never lose sight of its other kinds of evil. It is important to note that, in my view, there is no religious evil in nature or of nature as a whole to be contrasted with its religious goodness, but there are other kinds of evil in it that command our frank recognition. Nature's ambiguities are painfully apparent in these manifestations of evil.

In order to distinguish the religious goodness of nature from the evils it also contains, I shall henceforth use the term *rightness* (and its adjectival form *right*) to refer to the fundamental religious worth I am claiming for nature as a whole. And I shall reserve the terms *good* (or *goodness*) and *evil* to refer to aspects of nature for which these designations are appropriate. Hence, *there is no religious wrongness of nature to be contrasted with its religious rightness*, but there are evils in it to be contrasted with its goods.

When I speak of the religious rightness of nature, I am referring to its splendid appropriateness as the object of wholehearted religious reverence and devotion. Nature is fully entitled to this reverence and devotion, and hence is *religiously right* in its mixed character of nature natured and nature naturing. It is so entitled, not merely in spite of the ambiguities this intermingled character entails, but because of these ambiguities. The ambiguities are inevitable in the distinct faces or forms of what nature is now, has formerly been, and will forever become. They are inevitable because nature as I conceive it is a processive, ever-changing, ever-evolving system and series of such systems, whether viewed within the span of any particular period of time or over epochs of infinitely unfolding cosmic time. Nature thus understood is an inexorable blend of permanence and change, continuity and novelty, creation and destruction, order and disorder, oneness and manyness—and, yes, good and evil—so long as the last two terms are not taken to imply anything religiously inappropriate, religiously undesirable, or religiously deficient in value.

In this chapter I want to explore in some depth the ambiguities of nature, ambiguities that include both moral and systemic goods and evils. In the following chapters I shall explain why, despite its ambiguities and even precisely because of them, the whole of nature merits description as *unqualifiedly right* in the religious sense of that term and thus as an appropriate focus of religious commitment. In the process of doing so, I shall explicate the critically important notion of a distinctively religious species of value and compare and contrast it with what I deem to be most distinctive about the category of moral value. I shall also respond to the frequently heard objection that natural disasters should not be termed "evils." I believe strongly that they should, and I shall explain why.

Most importantly, I want to discuss at length the problem of how advocates of religion of nature can live with confidence and hope in the face of such ambiguities of nature as the appalling crimes, cruelties, and moral failings of some of its human creatures—conjoined with the exemplary deeds of justice, benevolence, and sympathy often routinely performed by others—and the frightening and sometimes horrifying effects of nature's devastations and destructions—existing alongside its sustaining and rejuvenating powers and the majesty and splendor of its creative processes. As we noted earlier, this problem is not just one for religion of nature or other kinds of religious naturalism. It is a problem for all religions and for secular outlooks and ways of life as well. No human being or human society can escape having to find ways to symbolize, conceptualize, and cope with the problem of the evils of the world in their relations to its goods. My focus in this book is on the specific resources of religion of nature for dealing with this problem.

NATURE AS A COINCIDENCE OF OPPOSITES

The title of this section is taken from a phrase used by the late Medieval philosopher Nicholas Cusanus (1401–1464) in his book *Of Learned Ignorance* (Cusanus 1954). He used this phrase and its accompanying concept as a way of dealing with what appear to be blatant contradictions in certain theological ideas. These ideas all center on the problem of how a *finite world* can be derived from, be supported by, and make manifest the existence, nature, and activity of an *infinite* God. We must, Cusanus contends, rise above Aristotle's familiar law of noncontradiction to a higher principle, namely, that of a coincidence of opposites (*coincidentia oppositorum*), in order to resolve the seeming contradictions posed by the notion—essential to theological thought—of the finite world's being somehow dependent upon and related to an infinite deity. I do not associate with Cusanus's phrase the specific theological meaning he gave it, but the phrase itself is a useful way of speaking of the ambiguities of nature, a nature displaying various kinds of profound oppositions that are nevertheless interwoven with one another.

What are these opposites? They include such things as creation and destruction, order and disorder, stability and change, causality and chance, plurality and unity, beauty and ugliness, the fixity of the past and openness of the future, continuity and freedom, evolutionary emergence and evolutionary extinction, life and death, disease and health, satiety and starvation, pleasure and pain, and moral goodness and evil. The oppositions of systemic natural goods and evils are implicit in some of the more detailed oppositions listed here. Nature is a place of joy and sorrow, contentment and anguish, fulfillment and frustration, confidence and uncertainty, hope and despair. It lacks dependable polish and smoothness. It bristles with rough edges. It keeps us off guard. It is a garden of delight but also a tangled wilderness of hazard and pain. Its gift of life is also a sentence of death. How can such opposites be reconciled? How can we make sense of nature and our place within it? How can we hope to find meaning for our lives in the face of nature's oppositions? How can something so obviously unstable and precarious, such a mishmash of goods and evils, be regarded as religiously right and a fit focus of religious faith?

TRYING TO IMAGINE A PERFECT WORLD

One way to think about these questions is to try to imagine a natural world radically different from the one in which we live, a world without risk or danger and devoid of any sort of ambiguity. Such a world would contain none of the systemic natural evils that we have talked about, and its human creatures would neither commit nor permit moral evils of any kind. It would be unqualifiedly good in all of its aspects and would lack no possible or pertinent goods. In a word, it would be a *perfect* world. It might seem obvious that such a world would be much more deserving of reverence, devotion, and trust than the present world I am proposing as a suitable object of religious faith. We will find reason presently to question this assumption, but let us continue trying to imagine a perfect world free of all traces of ambiguity.

The allegedly perfect natural world would need to be static and unchanging, or at least not exhibit any unexpected changes, in order to be entirely free of danger. A world without change, and especially life without change, is of course difficult to conceive. If this world did undergo change, all its changes would need to be benign so that none of nature's creatures could be hurt by them. It is hard to imagine how this could be possible, given that physical processes and entities have obdurate traits that can inflict harm. If the changes were not always benign, they would have to be not only knowable but known in advance to the last detail, so that living beings could anticipate them at all times and avoid being injured by them. Hence, there could be no such thing as novelty, unpredictability, or surprise in such a world. It would have to be causally determined in its every detail and run with the smooth precision of a fine machine. And its living beings would presumably have to be parts of that machine, running with the same smooth precision.

Not only would such a world contain no possibility of hazard or risk; there would also be no such thing as scarcity of resources, hunger or thirst, pain, suffering, diseases, accidents, mutilations, or malformations of birth. No sentient being would prey upon any other sentient being. All nature's creatures would live together in a peaceable kingdom of uninterrupted concord. If any sort of rivalry did exist, it would be a good-natured "win-win" rivalry amid abundant resources, with no loss for any creature of material or other kinds of good. No creature would suffer in the slightest degree or be put at the slightest disadvantage in relation to other creatures.

Evolution as we know it would be impossible in such a world, for there would no competition for scarce resources, no struggle for existence, and no extinctions. All of the biological species would have to be in place from the very beginning of such a world, if it is presumed to have had a beginning. Moreover, there could be no such thing as death in this imagined perfect world. Some very basic things about the world would have to be fundamentally different from what they are now in order for it either to accommodate or avoid an exponentially increasing number of newborn creatures that would otherwise exceed its supply of natural resources and even its spatial dimensions. Maybe the perfect world would not be spatial, in which case there would be no such thing as limitations of space, or maybe it could somehow expand spatially with its ever-increasing populations. Alternatively, perhaps there would be no births in this world; perhaps all of its individual immortal creatures, as well as their respective species, would be present in it from the beginning and never reproduce.

This imagined world, which we are requiring to be unambiguously good in every respect and every detail, would be devoid of any kind of human moral misdeed, however slight or heinous, and whether committed by mistake, neglect, or deliberate intent. All its human beings without exception would do only good and never evil. No goods would have to be sacrificed for the sake of other goods, and humans would be capable of comprehending with complete exactitude and certainty the distinctions between the possible goods and possible evils in every situation. Having no selfish impulses or destructive passions, and knowing full well the general, long-term benefits of the good and hurtful effects of the evil, they would never even be tempted to do evil. This world would contain no oppositions among humans, no struggles, no conflicts, and no regrettable choices. There would be no intermingling of moral goods and evils of any kind, and hence no moral ambiguities.

The natural world in this vision would be absolutely serene and se-cure—a blissful place of uninterrupted contentment and delight. There would be no pains or tears, no insecurities or dangers, no fears or vulnerabilities, no cruelty or hate, no mistakes or misapprehensions, no wars or oppres-sions. All possible goods would be attained at any given time, meaning that there would be no such thing as a conflict of goods or the need to choose between a lesser of two evils. Such a world would be a heaven on earth. Humans have yearned for something like it for millennia, assuming that this is the kind of world in which they would most want to live, swaddled in everlasting happiness and peace.

MISSING GOODS IN THE IMAGINED WORLD

We have to wonder, however, whether the imagined perfect natural world we have just described is even conceivable. It runs counter to almost every aspect of the world as we experience it, and in my attempt at a description of a perfect world rid of all traces of ambiguity, I have suggested some ways in which it would require such radical alterations as to be almost, if not entirely, beyond imagining. Its changes could never pose dangers or produce harm, for example. Its spatiality would either have to be fundamentally altered or this world could allow for no new births. There would never be conflicts of impulse, preference, or desire among any of its creatures, despite their individualities and diversities. No goods would have to be sacrificed for the sake of alternative goods, and distinctions between good and evil would be crystal clear in all situations. Not only humans but all this world's creatures would have to have absolute knowledge so as to predict the future with certainty, in order to avoid mistaken judgments or actions, to stay out of harm's way, and to discern with complete surety the differences between good and evil as these differences might pertain to themselves and all oth-ers. The machine-like predictability and regularity of this imagined world would not permit of any significant element of creativity, novelty, or change. Would time itself still be an intelligible conception? I doubt that it would and have argued to this effect elsewhere (D. A. Crosby 2005a). Perhaps a clever science fiction writer could make more sense out of such a world than I can. But I must confess that it stretches my imagination beyond its breaking point.

Let us grant, though, for the sake of argument that such a world might be conceivable. A further and even more important question is whether it would actually be desirable. Would we, upon due reflection, really *want* to live in the so-called perfect world, free of the least taint of ambiguity, I have tried to imagine? If not, then there must be something wrong with that world, something that should cause us to question its assumed perfection. I believe that there are serious deficiencies in such a world that make it far less desirable than we might initially have thought. A way for us to bring this idea into focus is to think about what would be missing in the imagined world.

What would be missing are a number of highly significant and desirable goods, showing that the perfect world has to eliminate these goods in order to achieve its own kinds of imagined good. Are its imagined goods worth the goods that would have to be eliminated? Is the supposed eradication of ambiguity worth its costs? If not, then we can begin to view our own ambiguous world with chastened vision and to appreciate from a fresh perspective the goods that are inseparable from its ambiguities.

It is important also to note that the imagined world cannot substantiate its claim to contain all possible goods, given that it must of necessity abandon many important goods in order to have its own kinds of good. Hence, its supposedly unalloyed, unqualified perfection must be questioned from this angle as well. I'll state my own claim in this regard as boldly as I can: *reality and ambiguity go necessarily together.* Any reality available to and intelligible for the likes of us is going to be in significant respects a coincidence of opposites. Without this coincidence, the concept of reality evaporates into something like the murky Undifferentiated Sphere—soaring above spatial differentiation, temporal change, or sensate experience—of the ancient philosopher Parmenides, for example, or the dizzying speculative heights of the eternal unity and sole reality of Idealistic philosophy's Absolute Spirit. We can understand this outcome more clearly when we consider some of the goods that are lost in the supposedly perfect world we tried to conceive.

There is the good of creativity, for example. We have shown that it would have to be absent in the imagined world. Nature's creations are bought at the price of its destructions. The one cannot be had without the other. Just as there would be nothing to destroy without nature's creations, there would be none of its creations without concomitant destructions. There is no ex nihilo creation in nature. Creation is always *transformation*, meaning that something of the old must be left behind in order that something new be brought into being. Time itself exhibits this dialectic. Were the past as past not left behind, there would be neither present nor future. And were every detail of the past carried over into the present, there would be no distinction between past and present. The new is purchased at the price of the old. Without this necessary loss in the passage of time, creativity would be impossible. Creativity and newness, on the one hand, and destruction and loss, on the other, are closely conjoined. Our world is a dynamic, ever-changing world. Only in such a world is genuine creativity possible.

Similarly, the profusion of diverse life forms we witness on earth today is an awesome good. We delight in the variety of creatures, with their distinct habits, skills, strategies, and niches, and the astounding range of their types, sizes, plumages, coats, vocalizations, wings, fins, limbs, hoofs, antennae, armor, speed, camouflage, and the like. This diversity is made possible not only by evolutionary developments but by massive evolutionary extinctions of species and regular deaths of individuals within those species, all of which would be absent in the imagined world. We ourselves are one of the diverse species and products of evolution. Life and death, evolution and extinction, are therefore correlative. And with life comes the capacity to feel, to sense, to be aware. These are also uncontestable goods. But these goods are conjoined with the capacity to experience pain, to suffer, to grieve, to know danger, to be anxious about how to protect oneself and one's kin. The good of being a rock does not require the bad of suffering, but the good of being alive and sensate necessarily includes susceptibility to it. To be capable of joy is also to be capable of pain.

Moreover, the good of a profusion of life forms means a plethora of demands placed upon the environment by the many different species and their individual members. These demands are not always compatible, they cannot always be satisfied in the maximal degree, and they often cannot even be partially satisfied without some amount of conflict, competition, and struggle—including the preying of one kind of life upon another kind. The resources of the environment themselves are threatened and limited by the ever-present pressure of new births and burgeoning populations, meaning that struggle for survival is inevitable. It is also the case that the fitness, balance, and survival of diverse species are heightened by conflict and competition. The weak and inept often fall by the wayside in order that the strong and their progeny—the fleet of foot, the cunning, the dexterous, the courageous—can ensure the long life line of a robust species or bring about the beginnings of new species. Sad as it is to say, diseases—often caused by the struggles of microscopic life forms for their own survival—and natural disasters of various kinds also have a winnowing role to play in maintaining a delicate balance of contending creatures and their needs, a balance that enables some numbers of them to remain alive and leave progeny, but at the expense of others. Systemic natural goods are not equally distributed among the creatures of nature.

The good of biological diversity thus brings in its train various kinds of systemic natural evils such as precarious conflicts and struggles, deprivation and pain, starvation and disease, death and extinction. Nature sustains its diverse creatures within themselves, in relation to one another, and in relation to the nonliving aspects of their environments, and it works constantly to bring new life forms into being. But in doing so it also allows some individuals to suffer and die, and whole species of them to cease to exist. The sufferings, deaths, and extinctions are not goods; they are intrinsic evils. But they make the good of biological diversity possible.

Another kind of good present in our world but not in the allegedly perfect imagined world is the good of genuine human freedom. The imagined world had to be causally determined so as to avoid anything happening to its creatures that could not be known in advance and thus threaten or endanger them by its unpredictability. But in a causally determined world, freedom is not possible. All its creatures are, as we saw, smoothly running machines, and nature functions there with machine-like precision. The price paid for this precision and complete predictability, and the safety and dependable regularity it provides, is the loss of freedom. The future is not open but closed. It contains but one possible, causally determined outcome at any given time. Alternative possible outcomes are not available for acts of freedom.

Of course, there are those who claim that our world is like this too, causally closed and determined in its every detail. But the claim itself and the reasons presented in support of it have meaning only if they are acts of free beings, not the rumblings of a preprogrammed machine. If determinism were true, there would be no clear way to know that it is true. We would not be in control of our own thoughts, and our discussions and debates about contested claims—including insistence upon the truth of complete causal determinism—would be nothing more than the pitting of one predetermined set of ideas against another. To be *caused* to believe something is different from being *justified* in believing it and *knowing* that one is justified in believing it in light of alternatives available for one's reflective reasoning and choice. Lacking freedom, we would be completely at the mercy of our impulses, prejudices, and desires, unable to distinguish what we might deeply want to be true, or are strongly impelled to regard as true, from what is true. Hence, it is not at all clear that in the imagined world there could be any such thing as the kind of critical thinking that presupposes an ability to choose rationally between justified and unjustified beliefs.

The imagined world appears to be a world of secure robots, not that of fully conscious and responsible, even if sometimes endangered, beings living in a complex, many-faceted world. Such an imagined world does not allow for free inquiry into the grounds of reliable truth and for free, open, and meaningful debate about contending claims. If I lacked freedom, I could not write this book, at least not in the way I conceive myself to be writing it. I might be a robot spinning out a predetermined program, in which case my thinking and that of all other human beings would be tales told by idiots. The tales might contain aspects of intelligence and wisdom, but we would be idiots with no way of knowing this to be the case, no ability to separate the chaff of falsehood from the wheat of truth.

The good of freedom not only requires a loose-limbed world with an open future, as opposed to a tightly bound, causally determined world. It also implies the ability to choose between moral goods and moral evils. The potentiality and high probability of moral evil are therefore contained within the good of freedom. Not to have the ability to commit evil acts would be to have a freedom without significant alternatives and without significant consequences. This would be a curious kind of freedom, a freedom hardly worth the name. Evil acts on the part of human beings are not made totally explicable by their possession of freedom. Other factors are involved as well—indifference, greed, anger, hatred, prejudice, lust, jealousy, fear, mental illness, addiction, and the like. These factors can give humans predilections toward evil actions that are not easily constrained by their capacity for freedom of choice, especially when reinforced by such things as defective family backgrounds, corrupt institutions, influences of evil companions, or unwise earlier choices that produced deeply entrenched bad habits of the present. The psychology of evil doers, which include all of us, is complicated and often baffling.

We have trouble explaining our own evil deeds to ourselves, to say nothing of being able to explain the evil deeds of others. But more than scientifically explicable cause-effect relations are involved. We are free, and the two-edged sword of our freedom goes a long way in accounting for the presence of moral evils in ourselves and in the world. Evil choices jeopardize the peace, security, and serenity of the world, and the results are sometimes horrible to behold. The innocent are often among the first victims of these evil choices. Even so, a total absence of moral evil, one characteristic of the ideal world we tried to imagine, would require the total absence of genuine freedom. Ambiguity is built into the gift of freedom; there is no such thing as freedom for the good that is not also freedom for the bad.

There is also a rather simplistic notion of moral good built into the imagined world. This is the idea that distinctions between moral good and moral evil are always black and white, with no shades of grey. Thus, no goods would have to be sacrificed for the sake of other goods. There would be no need for choice, in any situation, between lesser and greater evils. There would be no situation in which I might have to harm one person in order to save other persons from harm. There would be no irreconcilable conflicts between the goods of nonhuman organisms or other aspects of nonhuman nature and the goods of human beings and their economies and societies—irreconcilable in the sense of having to bring even the slightest detriment, harm, or damage to the one in order to avoid harm or procure good for the other. There would be no uncertainty about how to balance long-range good with presently attainable good. There would be no remorse over mistaken moral judgments of the past, because there would be no such mistakes.

This all sounds preposterous, but it would seem to be a necessary condition for the imagined world being free of any taint of moral evil. Only in such a world would the carefully considered, sometimes painfully unsure judgments of free beings not be required. Only in such a world would there be no such thing as regret about losses of good or about inflictions of evil required to bring about certain kinds of good. There would be no need for probabilistic reasoning in morals because there would be no such thing as in-principle situational uncertainties about what are the best moral choices to make in a given context. The law of excluded middle could be applied with ease to every moral problem. There would be no need for the less and more; all moral situations would be either-or. Morally correct choices could therefore be formalized and carried out without flaw by automated beings.

But as our experience so clearly shows us, the contending needs, demands, and alternatives of moral situations involving diverse beings do not always admit of such ready solutions. Most of the richness and complexity of moral situations in our world would have to be absent in the imagined world. This would be another price to be paid for its exclusion of human freedom in order to avoid freedom's risks, uncertainties, and dangers, and to guarantee the reign of absolute, unqualified moral goodness. Richness, complexity, and ambiguity in moral situations imply the need for subtlety of judgment in the face of uncertainty, and for the fallible resources and strategies of deliberative freedom.

I am claiming that the ideal world we sought earlier to imagine would necessarily lack certain goods of our present world. The fact that it would have to lack these goods shows that the ideal world could not be a compendium of all possible goods and thus that it would not be perfect in that sense of the term. So far, I have indicated what three of the crucially important missing goods would have to be, goods that can be present only in an ambiguous world such as our own. These goods, as we saw, are creativity, a profuse diversity of life forms, and human freedom. Each of these missing goods is ambiguous in that it implies the accompaniment of certain kinds of evil.

The systemic natural good of creativity implies the systemic natural evil of destruction, for example, because transformative creativity and destruction go necessarily together. The systemic natural good of an ever-evolving profusion of life forms means such systemic natural evils as suffering, starving, succumbing to disease, being the victim of predation, death itself, and the extinctions of species. The good of human freedom allows for the possibility and probability of moral evil as well as for moral goodness, and thus for all of the deplorable effects of moral evil.

We also noted that the absence of freedom entailed by the imagined security of a completely determined world would mean absence of the good of critical reflection, a mode of thinking and acting that is able to distinguish justified from unjustified claims to truth and that can freely and rationally opt for the first as over against the second. And we saw that exclusion of the good of freedom, combined with the claim to total moral goodness in the imagined world, would mean that the imagined world could not contain the richness and complexity of moral situations—or of moral possibilities—in our world. All its moral situations would have to be implausibly simple and dichotomous, with no need for the subtle, risky, difficult judgments of deliberative freedom. This would be a markedly flat, uninteresting, unexciting world, hardly a suitable home for creatures such as ourselves.

Nature's rightness, therefore, need not connote for humans or its other creatures uninterrupted happiness, seamless harmony, absence of conflict, complete confidence about the future, lack of struggle, sorrow, or pain. It need not require that nature be a Pleasantville or paradise of everlasting pleasure and contentment. If nature were these things, many of the goods that we cherish in human life would be impossible. I have discussed three of these goods. Here is a brief indication of some other important goods and the tensions and ambiguities they imply. There can be no courage without risk and danger. And we greatly admire courage. There can be no joy of attainment in difficult tasks without struggle. My students sometimes complain that philosophy is too hard. I respond that if a philosophical problem is not hard and demanding, sometimes to the point of desperation, it is probably not worth attending to. The pleasure of doing philosophy stems from the extreme difficulty of most of its problems and the satisfaction of making some progress, however small, in trying to solve them. The same is true of many other difficult but highly worthwhile endeavors and activities. The seamless harmony of the imagined perfect world would mean the absence of dialectical tension, challenge, and disagreement, and thus of the hope of deeper insight and fulfillment. It would mean the lack of a diversity of outlooks and points of view without which we would soon become smug and too easily satisfied with our own limited ways of thinking.

If there were no failures and disappointments, we could not learn from their lessons. We are instructed as much, if not more, by our frustrations and failures as by our satisfactions and successes. Temperance would be pointless were there no passions leading toward extremes. Effort would be pointless without obstacles. Honor would be meaningless were there no temptations to dishonorable actions and no difficulty in attaining an honorable character. Love, compassion, and justice would merit no praise were there no contending impulses toward indifference, selfishness, bigotry, or hate.

Nature's rightness pertains not just to our species but to all species of earth. So we humans are not its sole focus or its only beneficiary. And its processes apply not just to earth but to the universe as a whole. So we will usually but not always benefit from nature's workings, just as is the case for other earthly species. What is right is for us to affirm our lowly place in the whole scheme of things and to be thankful that we can be participants in this scheme, with the inestimable gifts of sentience, conscious awareness, and freedom. We are at home in the universe, but the consequence of being at home is that we are subject to the forces and powers of nature just as its other creatures are. We can mitigate the harmful powers of nature to some extent with our technological knowledge and prowess, and we are often entitled and obligated to do so. But we cannot expect to be masters of nature or to insulate ourselves completely from its potential harms. Humility and gratitude should be our watchwords, not arrogance or resentment.

I trust that the observations and arguments up to this point in the chapter are relevant and worth pondering, but they do not plumb the depths of potential and actual evil in processes of the nonhuman world or in human actions. They tend to leave us on too high a plane of abstraction and may suggest too romanticized a view of nature. It is one thing to talk about the ravages of evil and to explore them conceptually. It is quite another to experience them at firsthand. In claiming religious rightness for nature despite its systemic and moral evils, I want to be sure to emphasize that the full range of its evils is meant, including dreadful evils that many people—especially those in prosperous, relatively safe communities and circumstances—might be untouched by throughout their lives. We turn next, therefore, to samples of monstrous evils of the two types, beginning with systemic natural evil. This sampling can help to make us more fully aware of the ominous evils included, along with manifest goods, in nature's ambiguities and of the stringent test these evils pose for confidence in nature's religious rightness.

RAVAGES OF SYSTEMIC NATURAL EVIL

In this section I present two examples of the shocking and terrible devastation that can result from what I am calling systemic natural evils. The first example is the great influenza pandemic that swept across the world in 1918–19 and killed at least twenty-five million people. Some estimates place the number of deaths even higher, perhaps as high as twice or four times that number. The people of entire villages perished in Alaska and southern Africa, and populations in a number of towns elsewhere in the world were also wiped out. Mass graves had to be dug in some places to bury the dead. Individuals with no prior symptoms would be suddenly stricken with the disease, experience pervasive weakening of their bodies within hours, and die the next day. Initially mild cases of the flu would often turn quickly into vicious cases of pneumonia. People would desperately gasp for air as fluid filled their lungs, and bloody froth would issue from their mouths and noses before they expired.

Influenza is usually most deadly for the extremely young and the elderly, but in this pandemic those in the twenty-five to thirty-four year age group were extensively affected as well. The virus responsible for this unspeakable horror is now thought to have been of the H1 virus type. The pandemic vanished after about eighteen months. As many, if not more, persons had been killed by it when it was over as had died on both sides in the tragic carnage of the just concluded World War I. The rapid spread of the epidemic around the globe was probably abetted by the massing of

armies and their transportation in ships and other conveyances in the last
phase of the war, as well as by large groups of people gathering together to
celebrate the war's end.[1] A stark lesson of the precarious fragility of human
life and its susceptibility to harm and destruction by natural forces is taught
by this sudden, unpredicted, immense onslaught of a disease whose causes
were unknown by the medical science of the time. Wives, husbands, children,
brothers, sisters, other family members, friends, colleagues, and neighbors
were cut down by the disease and bemoaned by those who survived. One
of my father's brothers was its victim in his late teens.

Our natural home is not just a serene countryside cottage, although
it may often seem like that as we wander in a quiet wood, sit beside a sea-
side with gently rolling waves, or enjoy the untroubled exuberance of good
health. It is also a place of turbulent, sometimes unexpected and disastrous
changes affecting humans and other aspects of the natural environment.
The changes may come over a relatively short period of time, as was the
case in the pandemic of 1918–19. But sometimes they may take hundreds
or thousands of years to develop, and then manifest themselves in sudden
widespread destruction. Such is the case with our second example of natural
systemic evil, a stupendous earthquake and its accompanying tsunami of
December 26, 2004. The earthquake, estimated to be between magnitude
9.15 and 9.3 on the Richter scale, making it the second largest earthquake
ever recorded on a seismograph, took place deep within the Indian Ocean
about 150 miles off the coast of Sumatra. It was the result of the slow but
relentless movement of a lower tectonic plate carrying India being forced or
subducted beneath an upper plate carrying most of South-East Asia. Unlike
most earthquakes, which last but a few seconds, this one lasted nearly ten
minutes and caused the whole planet to vibrate.

The tremors of the earthquake gave rise to a tsunami that impacted
the shores of Indonesia, Sri Lanka, South India, and Thailand with multiple
colossal waves, and caused serious damage and deaths as far as the east
coast of Africa. The resultant death toll of humans has been estimated to
be around 265,000, with tens of thousands more missing and more than a
million left homeless. Many of the missing were never found because they
were carried out to sea. Relief agencies reported that about one-third of
the deaths were children. There were poignant tales of children who ran
down to the beach to enjoy the spectacle of fish left flapping on the beach
by the water's receding a mile or more prior to the strike of the tsunami.
The children were swept away by millions of tons of sea water in waves
sixty feet or more in height. They were tossed, torn, and suffocated by the
monstrous fury of the waves. The waves reached as far as a half-mile inland
in some places, wreaking havoc on everything in their path. Salt water
intruded into aquifers and wells, and rendered agricultural areas sterile.
Homes, stores, schools, factories, and sewer systems were destroyed. Huge
ships were tossed onto the land.

It was not only human beings whose lives and livelihoods were wiped out by the earthquake and tsunami. Severe damage was inflicted on ecosystems, with their vegetation and animals. Mangroves, coral reefs, forests, coastal wetlands, dunes, rock formations, and groundwater were affected. Solid and liquid wastes and industrial chemicals spread by the tsunami threatened the environment as well. The inrush of salt water damaged delicate ecosystems in fresh bodies of water or ones in incremental stages between salt and fresh. The whole island of Simueleu, close to the quake's epicenter, was *tilted* by the force of the earthquake, causing pristine underwater ecosystems to be exposed.[2] If ever a reminder is needed that we human beings are not the lords of earth or centers of the universe, and that our lives, along with the lives of countless other living beings, are relatively small and insignificant within the whole vast scheme of an ever-changing nature, the tsunami of December 2004 was such a reminder.

Contemplating these two examples of natural systemic evils can help to bring home to our sympathies and imaginations, and not just to our abstract conceptualizations, the kinds of horrifying devastation that can result from natural forces, forces that pay little heed to our human lives and concerns or to other natural beings caught up within them. These forces are astonishingly creative but can also be massively destructive.

We can now address the question posed in an earlier part of this chapter: Is it appropriate to refer to such devastations of nature as "evils"? I am convinced that it is appropriate to do so, and I want now to indicate why. It is true that in the outlook of religion of nature the forces of nature are blind, in the sense of not being intended by any conscious agent and therefore not being directed toward any kind of envisioned end. They are not acts of God, for example, or things allowed by God to take place for whatever reasons God might have in mind. Thus, they are not evil in the way that a crime committed by a human being can be said to be evil. There is no malice aforethought involved, no malignant intentionality or purpose. In a word, such events are not *moral* evils, evils for which we could hold a conscious, purposeful being culpable.

Why, then, call them evil? Events of nature are evil, in my view, when they cause suffering, deprivation, or death to sentient beings. They are intrinsically bad from the perspectives of these beings, no matter how they may be seen from other perspectives. And it is not just effects of major natural disasters that we are entitled to brand as evil. Each victim of starvation, thirst, freezing, drowning, burning, predation, and the like experiences a kind of evil, no matter how routine or natural in a larger perspective those experiences may be said to be. When experienced by human beings, effects of the destructive forces of nature are regarded as something undeniably painful, horrible, and regrettable—something rightfully termed evil because of the great harm of these effects upon themselves, upon those whom they love, or upon other humans. They also qualify as evil in environmentally sensitive human perspective when they wreak havoc on ecosystems and nonhuman life forms.

A strong word is needed to characterize such experiences and happenings. It is not enough for us to look on and say, "But it's just the ways of nature. These ways have no values or disvalues in and of themselves. They may seem unfortunate, but basically they just *are*, and that is the end of the matter." As we shall see in a later chapter in which I present outlines of a perspectivist metaphysics and its implications, reality is a congeries of perspectives and their constituents. There is no way in which a thing can simply be, in and of itself, independently of all perspectives or outside of all contexts of relation. Just as to *be* is to be the constituent of a perspective and to be in relation to other perspectives, to be *good or evil* is to be such from a perspective or set of perspectives. I do not mean to suggest that all such perspectives are equally correct or justified, only that good or evil are such in relation to some perspective or other. I discuss this point in more detail in chapter 4. A supposedly completely neutral or wholly objective perspective, devoid of relativities and relations implied by other actual or possible perspectives, would be a contradiction in terms, an alleged *non-perspectival perspective*.

Thus, there can be no such thing as isolated, unrelated, purely in-itself being or value. From the perspectives of those who suffer severely from the effects of natural occurrences—from such things as disease, disaster, deprivation, or death—these occurrences can be so fraught with threat, disruption, and loss as justly to be seen as evil. It makes no difference to say that from other perspectives these occurrences might not be regarded as evil. It is good for predators to find their prey, for example, because predation is necessary to preserve their lives and the lives of their progeny. But the process of being killed and eaten is evil from the perspective of the ones being preyed upon and from the standpoint of their progeny, now left defenseless and unprotected. Both perspectives are real or aspects of the real. Such events and their consequences are not just ways of nature to be dismissed with a wave of the hand as neutral with respect to value or disvalue. They can be glaringly evil in their impression and effect upon beings capable of suffering and pain. To assume or argue that they are neither good nor evil *in themselves* is to take issue with the perspectivist metaphysics I shall later defend in more detail.

Our firm answer to the question "Why call some systemic natural occurrences evil?" leads to another one that shall occupy us throughout this book. That question is, "How can a nature so pervaded by these kinds of systemic natural evil—if we agree to call them that—be regarded as religiously right, as deserving of a lifetime of religious devotion?" I shall take up that question in due course. But let us turn now to the moral evils of nature—the evils committed or allowed by human beings—as further evidence of nature's pervasive ambiguity. Here again, we shall look at two striking and extreme examples so as to emblazon on our minds the depths of moral evil we encounter in our world. Since we humans are creatures of nature, momentous moral evils are aspects of nature, the same nature I am upholding as the appropriate object of religious faith.

DEPTHS OF MORAL EVIL

The two examples of moral evil I present in this section are different in character. The first one describes the training of soldiers by the militaristic Japanese government—and the subsequent actions of these soldiers—at the time of the Japanese invasions of East Asia beginning in the 1930s and up through World War II. This is an example of consciously planned and enacted institutional evil and its horrendous influences upon the actions of individuals within an institution. The second example involves an individual acting entirely on his own without institutional sanction or support. This individual was affected by influences, limitations, and failures of his surrounding institutions as we all are, but his evil actions did not result from conscious malicious planning on the part of leaders of an institution in the way that the actions of the Japanese soldiers did.

In what follows, I do not intend to analyze individual psychological causes or motives underlying the moral evils in either case. This is certainly a subject of great importance, but to undertake an investigation of its complexities would carry us too far from the main purpose of this book. What I want to do is to cite these two cases as examples to be pondered of the deplorable depths of moral evil to which societies and individuals can stoop and the appalling consequences of such evil.

With cases such as these in view, as well as ones akin to the two examples of systemic natural evils already discussed, we should be able to rid our minds of any tendency to underestimate, gloss over, or sentimentalize the radical ambiguities of nature. These cases should also make starkly apparent our obligation to struggle to eliminate or at least to mitigate the devastating effects of such evils to the fullest extent of our powers. Recognition of the ineliminable ambiguities of nature does not entitle us to attitudes of wholesale resignation, apathy, or despair. Even though our previous arguments show that an intricate admixture of actual and possible goods and evils will always be present, we should fight continually to counterbalance the evils with as much good as we can help to secure in the world.

We also need to remind ourselves that the term *ambiguities* connotes moral goods as well as moral evils, and that systemic natural goods, and not just evils, are included in these ambiguities as well. Nature incorporates innumerable astounding goods of both types, and I shall want to do justice to this welcome fact in the next chapter and the ones to follow. But let me now direct attention to the first of the two examples of moral evil I want us to consider.

By the time the Japanese emperor Hirohito ascended his throne in 1926, Japan had become an obsessively militaristic state. Hirohito himself had received a military education and was thoroughly indoctrinated in the outlooks and policies of that state. He was also made an officer in both the imperial Japanese army and navy. The military leaders were in complete control of civic aspects of the government, and they also controlled the education of the young. Curriculum materials were suffused with celebrations of Japanese military might, and war and patriotism were stressed in every subject. Military-minded teachers did everything they could to prepare their pupils to serve the emperor in war, and the pupils were taught that they owed absolute obedience to the emperor and his military representatives. They were taught that there was no greater glory and honor than to die for the emperor in war, that war is brutal and they should not shrink from any cruelty or brutality required of them, and that they should subject themselves without question to the mandates of their superiors. They were told that these mandates were the emperor's own commands and that they possessed the infallibility of his status as a living god. Pupils in the schools were subjected to harsh discipline, and recruits in the army were routinely beaten, harassed, and humiliated while officers looked on laughing. The object was to mold students and soldiers into unthinking, unquestioning instruments of the Japanese militaristic state and its war machine. They were also imbued with an unquestioning conviction of the racial superiority and divinely appointed destiny of the Japanese people.

The military leaders soon began to call for expansion beyond Japan's shores. There were plenty of juicy examples of such expansion in the colonial policies and practices of the Western powers, especially those of Great Britain, a nation that had acquired territories around the globe. Japan wanted a piece of this action. It wanted to have its own colonial empire in East Asia and the Pacific, its own sphere of influence and control, and its own highly favorable trade arrangements within that sphere. In this way, Japan could be like the other colonial powers and a mighty island empire in the East similar to Great Britain in the West. Inspired by this vision, Japan invaded and occupied Manchuria in 1931 and launched a full-scale attack on China in 1937. In September 1940 it occupied northern Indochina, and in July 1941 it took over southern Indochina. Japan had already annexed Korea in 1910. Not content with encircling China, the Japanese turned their eyes toward the south Pacific, and the attack on the United States at Pearl Harbor in late 1941 was designed to cripple the United States Navy in order to prevent it from interfering with Japanese colonial designs on Malaya, Singapore, Indochina, and the Philippines.

Our concern here is with the shocking behavior of many members of the Japanese army in China after the invasion of 1937. This behavior was encouraged, supported, or countenanced by the Japanese government, by its official military policies, and by its military leaders. The fault is not only with the soldiers who perpetrated crimes against the Chinese people but with the government that trained them and gave them license to do so. What were these crimes? Some of them were an integral part of the training of Japanese soldiers. Others related to treatment of prisoners of war in battle, and still others related to treatment of civilians in Chinese villages and towns.

A central part of the training regime for Japanese officers and enlisted men in occupied China was a so-called trial of courage. Captive Chinese were brought before officers or enlisted men in training. They were blindfolded and tied with ropes. Officers were commanded to behead the captives one by one with army swords. Enlisted men were told to bayonet them. In the second case, a red circle would be drawn around the heart of the victim, and the enlisted men were ordered to avoid the heart when they plunged their bayonets into the captive. The rationale was to keep the captive alive as long as possible through successive bayonet attacks. The announced purpose of these macabre modes of "training" was to steel the hearts of the soldiers to acts of killing and to make them brave in battle.

Viewing Chinese lives as worthless, and with pride in their having been trained to have the courage to do so, some Japanese officers beheaded Chinese captives on a regular basis just to stay in practice for warfare and to exhibit their scorn for the enemy. There was even a contest reported in the Japanese newspapers between Lieutenant "M" and Lieutenant "N" to see which one could be the first to behead one hundred prisoners. Japan never formally declared war on China and refused to apply the constraints of international law on the treatment of prisoners of war. The Japanese scorned soldiers who surrendered in war, regarding them as cowardly and dishonorable, and showed no hesitation in starving them, torturing them, killing them outright, or forcing them into slave labor. The Japanese treatment of prisoners led to the deaths of one in four, or perhaps even one in three of them overall.

When it came to civilians, the treatment was no less callous and brutal. Orders to troops were that they had to obtain food locally. No supplies would be coming from the rear. This entitled soldiers to take from villagers, already growing barely enough to feed themselves, whatever food they wanted. Village men were hunted down and killed, regardless of whether or not there was any evidence of their being involved with the Chinese army. Whole villages were torched. Women were raped at will and then killed. Others became sex slaves, forced into military brothels to be used for the pleasure of the troops. Virgins between the ages of twelve and fifteen were especially desired, since they could be assumed to be free of sexually transmitted diseases. Babies were tossed into the air and impaled on bayonets for fun or thrown into vats of water or oil. People were doused with gasoline and set afire. Sticks of dynamite were shoved up girls' vaginas to blow them up. When troops were hungry for meat and none was available, Chinese captives were carved up and the meat of their bodies roasted for food. The Japanese also engaged in ghoulish experiments to devise methods of biological warfare, killing numerous humans in the experiments and wiping out hundreds of thousands of Chinese people by inflicting upon them diseases such as anthrax, typhoid, and plague. The horrible list of atrocities goes on.

Enough has been said about this example of the Japanese government, military leaders, and soldiers to drive home the general point that the depths of institutionally supported moral evils carried out by members of institutions on their behalf and in their name cannot be fathomed. It is not only the Japanese, of course, who have committed such atrocities in time of war or at other times. I do not want to suggest that they alone were guilty of such crimes or even that their crimes—brutal as they were—are the worst on record. I cite their actions as a single glaring example of the indisputable fact that institutionally sanctioned moral evils have long been part of the history of humankind, and that many of these evils have been unspeakably vicious and horrible.

We could also have talked about Stalin's rampant political executions, the starving of millions of peasants resulting from his collectivist policies, or the treatment of individuals sent to his gulags. We could have spoken of Hitler's demonic and crazed persecution of millions of Jewish men, women, and children. We could have brought into consideration the merciless Allied firebombings of cities such as Dresden and Tokyo toward the end of World War II in its European and Pacific theaters. Surely the latter must have seemed like atrocities from the perspective of those subjected to them. This was likely to have been so from their perspective, however justified the bombings may have seemed to Allied planners intent upon bringing about an end to the stupendous evils of two totalitarian regimes bent upon ruthless domination of their respective parts of the world. This last example shows the ineliminable ambiguity of some moral situations: in order to eliminate one evil, another evil must be committed. The choice is not simply between evil and good, but between greater and lesser evils in order to achieve whatever good one can. And the lesser evil may be horrible in its own right. Or we could have detailed atrocities committed by people of the United States against Native Americans, such as the massacre by a contingent of the United States Cavalry of defenseless Cheyenne and Arapaho children, women, and old men at Sand Creek, Colorado, in 1864, or the often callous, racist, and unfeeling treatment of Filipino freedom fighters and non-combatants by American soldiers in the war to acquire the Philippines (1899–1902).[3]

The second example of moral evil I want to bring into view is one conveyed to me by word of mouth. I do not use any names, but my narrative is based upon facts. A husband and wife who became foster parents for two little girls, one three and the other six, were told that the girls had been regularly molested sexually by a boyfriend of their mother, apparently with the mother's consent. The children were afraid to go asleep at night, because they had been awakened on many occasions by the boyfriend to be used for his sexual pleasure. When a man would come into the room, they would instinctively go over to place their heads in his crotch, because they thought this was how they should relate to men. Their language was laced with sexual explicatives we would not expect from the mouths of children. The two children were developmentally delayed in language usage and social behavior.

It is hard to conceive of a starker, more glaring, and more disgusting form of moral evil than the behavior of the boyfriend and its effects upon the children. He corrupted these children and placed burdens on their psyches at critical points in their development. It will probably take a lifetime of torment and struggle for them to cope with these burdens. This kind of case is not isolated. It occurs again and again in our society and other societies, and its consequences for the lives of children throughout their lives are unimaginably destructive and dire. Those who perpetrate this kind of evil are free, and they are responsible for the terrible misuses of their freedom, whatever their own backgrounds or past experiences may have been. This is not to say that they deserve no compassion—they may themselves have been sexually abused or badly treated in other ways in their own childhoods—but it is to say that they cannot escape responsibility for their actions. People who perform such deeds are integral parts of nature, and the possibility and actuality of their flagrant immorality is part of the ambiguity of nature we need frankly, if regretfully, to acknowledge. We could, of course, cite many other and different kinds of examples, but this one should suffice to make the point.[4]

In light of these poignant examples of systemic natural evils and appalling examples of moral evils—accompanied by sad recognition that the examples barely scratch the surface of the depths of evil displayed in the world—how can nature still qualify as a fit focus of religious faith? If it can, in what specific ways can it be claimed to do so? And what kind of response can be made to objections implicit in these examples against this book's claim for nature's unqualified religious rightness? In the next chapter, I turn to the positive side of the ledger of nature's ambiguities and begin to establish a case for its religious ultimacy in the face of its ambiguities.[5]

THREE

NATURE AS THE FOCUS
OF RELIGIOUS FAITH

Heaven is my father and earth is my mother, and even such a small thing as I finds an intimate place in their midst. Therefore, that which fills the universe I regard as my body, and that which directs the universe I regard as my nature. All people are my brothers and sisters, and all things are my companions.

—Chang Tsai (quoted by Tu Wei-Ming)

What is good about nature? "Everything," is my answer, at least if we mean religiously good. As I noted in chapter 1, there is no religious wrongness of nature in my version of religious naturalism. Nature is unqualifiedly right or good *in the distinctively religious connotations of these terms* and therefore richly deserving of our deepest reverence and devotion. This is so in spite of and even because of the systemic natural and moral ambiguities of nature we highlighted in the previous chapter. These ambiguities, indisputably real, threatening, and deplorable as they often are, involve two different senses of good in relation to two different senses of evil. But they do not diminish or detract from the religious rightness of nature I am defending here. I shall continue to argue in this chapter and the ones to follow that nature's ambiguities are not just traits of it we must begrudgingly resign ourselves to and learn to tolerate. And I contended in the previous chapter that we would be extremely reluctant, after due reflection, to be rid of them in some kind of imagined world. Its ambiguities are essential to nature's creativity, beauty, and sustaining power, and to the profound meaning and value a religion of nature can provide for human life.

In this chapter I first explain how I conceive of religious faith. I do this in order to make clear what I mean when I speak of centering one's faith on nature and committing one's life to it as religiously ultimate. Second, I elaborate and defend important respects in which nature is entitled to be the object of such faith. Third, I argue for the view that the *whole* of nature is inviolably holy or sacred and thus the fit object of faith, and not just some particular *aspect* of nature.

Discussion of this last topic will set the stage for the following chapter, in which I set forth and defend a version of metaphysical perspectivism in order to show not only the intricate interconnectedness of the multiple constituents and dimensions of nature but also their inescapable oppositions and tensions in relation to one another in the dynamic system that is nature. Perspectivism, pluralism, and ambiguity, I argue in that chapter, go necessarily together. It would therefore make no more sense to seek to orient one's faith around only a part of nature, given nature's ineluctably perspectival character, than it would for one of the women in King Solomon's judgment hall to settle for part of a baby in support of her claim to be the baby's mother.

CONCEPT OF RELIGIOUS FAITH

Religious faith is often thought to be an assent of the will to religious truth-claims that can neither be proved nor disproved on the basis of experience or reason. One assents to these claims, according to this view, because they are proposed for belief by persons, documents, traditions, or institutions that are alleged to have authority in such matters. The basis for one's assenting to these beliefs, therefore, is the authority of their source, not one's own deliberation or thought. Understood in this way, faith is altogether distinct from reason. Where reason cannot go or might seem to prohibit one from going, faith goes. Even something that might seem contradictory or absurd from the standpoint of reason can still be asserted and assented to by faith. Faith makes up for reason's deficiencies and limitations; it helps us to navigate among and to discern the truth of mysterious claims to truth that reason has no competency to judge. To accept something as true on the basis of faith is, then, to grit your teeth and resolve to believe it despite the lack of convincing evidence for its truth, the presence of seeming evidence against its truth, or its unintelligibility to the rational mind.

There are a number of things wrong with this concept of faith. For one thing, it makes the act of faith completely arbitrary. If experience and reason have no role in helping us to decide the authoritative sources in which we are to put our trust, which authorities should we rest our faith upon and why? In this concept, there is no explanation of why we should choose one authority over another one. All we can do is to surrender to what someone or something tells us is the truth. Were there no conflicting claims to religious truth, this would perhaps not be as much of a problem. But there are many different religious claims and allegedly authoritative sources of those claims. For another thing, this concept of faith supposes that one can believe in something as a sheer act of the will. But one cannot simply *will* to believe something. One must be *convinced* that something is true in order truly to believe it. And it is hard to understand how one could be convinced if the belief in question does not have plausibility or convincingness in its own right, apart from the authoritative source or sources to which appeal is made. A third problem with this concept of faith is its assumption that faith is merely an act of belief, an act of assenting to the truth of a proposition or set of propositions.

All of these assumptions are seriously deficient as interpretations of the meaning of faith. A completely arbitrary faith is a meaningless faith. It is like basing one's life on the spin of a roulette wheel or the toss of a coin. One cannot simply choose to believe something in the absence of any evidence for its truth and by blind appeal to some kind of external authority. "Why this putative authority rather than some other one?" is a question that goes unanswered. And the notion of simply being able to will oneself to believe something one has no rational or experiential basis to believe is implausible and odd. It makes no sense to think of being able to respond to a command to believe, and it makes no sense to command oneself to believe. One might act as if one believed, but that is a different matter. Finally, and perhaps most importantly, the life of faith is just that—a whole way of life—and not just the assertion of a claim or collection of claims as true. It involves mind, heart, and will, not just will alone, and it involves a lifetime of demanding commitment and practice, not just inward acts of mental assent.

Faith structures and orients one's existence. It is the act of the whole person, involving the whole of a person's life. To have religious faith, properly understood, is to stake one's life on something of momentous value and importance, and that level of commitment requires all the resources and capacities of one's being. Reliance on properly evaluated and carefully deliberated types of evidence is vitally relevant to a responsible life of faith. The final test of faith is the integration and wholeness it brings to every aspect of a person's life, and the positive contributions it motivates a person to make to the lives of others, both human and nonhuman. A viable faith should also be a source of inspiration and strength for communities and societies.

It will help to bring this concept of faith into clearer focus if we think about the following story. A novice clerk in a mountaineering store is waiting on a customer who wants to buy a rope for rappelling. There are three qualities of rope available. The customer does not want to spend a lot of money, so he asks if the lowest priced rope will be sufficient to hold him and not to fray, tear, or break as he rappels off steep, rocky cliffs in a remote wilderness. The clerk assures him that it will be sufficient, speculating to himself that the store would probably not sell the rope if it were not safe. The customer himself has had no experience with climbing ropes; he will be climbing with a more experienced friend.

It is one thing for the customer to will himself to assent to the proposition "This rope will be sufficient to hold you" on the authority of the clerk in the store and because of his wish not to spend much money. He wills to believe that the proposition is true, or at least he does so if we assume for the moment that the concept of faith we are holding up to critical scrutiny is credible. But when he gets out to the mountainside and tosses his new rope over a sheer precipice for the first time, he is in quite a different situation. It suddenly occurs to him that he will be committing *his life* to the rope. Now the issue is not just a proposition to be believed but a life to be risked—his own precious life!

He formerly believed something to be true about the rope, and he believed it largely on the basis of an external authority, the clerk in the store. He could be fairly nonchalant about the belief so long as the rope was lying on a shelf in his closet. But now he is in a situation where he has to have utmost confidence in the rope, confidence enough to stake his life upon its reliability. The former situation is one where mere belief could suffice, perhaps even arbitrarily willed belief, if that were possible. The latter situation calls for far more than that. It calls for a position of trust, assurance, and commitment from which one's very life hangs in the balance.

I am not suggesting that one can have *religious* faith in a rope, but I am trying to elucidate the difference between mere belief in a set of propositions propounded by religious authorities, no matter how tenaciously one holds to the belief qua belief, and the act of religious faith whereby one entrusts the whole of one's life to some kind of religious ultimate, whether it be Yahweh, Allah, the Triune God, Ahura Mazda, the Goddess, Shiva, the gods, Brahman, Nirvana, Tao, humanity, nature, or something else. The act of religious faith is literally a matter of life and death, since one is entrusting the whole of one's being to one specific path and pattern of life until one dies.

The philosopher Alfred North Whitehead sums up the nature of the religious quest and, by implication, the character of religious faith with this trenchant question: "What, in the way of value, is the attainment of life?" (Whitehead 1926:60). According to Whitehead, this question in various forms is asked by humans in their moods of solitariness as they brood on the deepest challenges and mysteries of existence and on what they can contribute out of their freedom and the resources of their individual existences to the betterment of the world. A satisfactory answer to the question cannot come from authorities outside oneself. It can only come from within, from the depths of one's own searching soul. Meaningful religious life can be instructed and informed by the experiences and insights of others, but it is authentic and truly fulfilling only when it is nurtured and confirmed by one's own reflections and brought to the continuing test of one's own firsthand experiences.[1]

Religious faith is therefore a matter of *being*, not just of believing. More is required for a genuine life of faith than mere volitional assent to propositions claimed to be authoritative but for which there is insufficient evidence or reasonableness in their own right, or than dogged affirmation of proposals for belief in the face of their seeming incredibility. Too much is at stake to rest content with this view of faith. Such so-called faith is a vice, not a virtue, despite its zealous endorsement by various religious persons and institutions. It preempts and even condemns critical reflection and development of personal responsibility. It encourages dishonesty about one's real commitments and beliefs by recommending unquestioning conformity to external authorities. It is a recipe for hypocrisy and inauthenticity, for pretending to affirm what one does not genuinely believe and for avoiding responsibility for how one thinks and what one becomes.

If followed through to its logical conclusion, advocacy of such blind, willful credulity in the name of religion is pernicious. It can give rise to the worst kinds of fanaticism, intolerance, and irrationalism, and it has continued to do so throughout human history. When I speak of nature as the focus of religious faith, I do not have in mind this weak and potentially dangerous conception—or, more properly, *misconception*—of faith. In the New Testament, Christians are admonished to "test the spirits to see whether they are of God" (I John 4: 1; RSV). Similarly, we should test the candidates for faith to see if they can hold up under the scrutiny of our reasoning powers and enable us to live effectively in the face of the sometimes arduous demands of life. I am convinced that there are persuasive reasons to place one's faith in nature as the religious ultimate to which one can devote one's life, and I want now to indicate some of these reasons.

DEFENSE OF RELIGION OF NATURE

"Religion of nature," it will be recalled, is the term I am using for the version of religious naturalism I am advocating and defending in this book. For religion of nature the appropriate focus of religious faith, as I characterized such faith in the previous section, is nature itself. There is thus no need for recourse to any kind of *super*natural principles, powers, presences, beings, or domains. What sort of case can be made for religion of nature as a type of religious outlook and practice and as a candidate for religious faith? This book as a whole is intended to provide convincing answers to this question.[2] However, in the present section we shall look at specific reasons in support of my contention as a proponent of religion of nature that ultimate importance, meaning, and value—and all that is required for a robust, demanding, and completely fulfilling religious life—can be found in nature. Here are the reasons.

1. If nature conceived as both nature natured (the present face of nature) and nature naturing (the creative powers underlying and transforming the

present face of nature over time) is *metaphysically* ultimate, that is, if there is nothing beyond or behind nature—nothing required to account for its existence or to uphold it in being—then this fact alone is reason to recognize it as being *religiously* ultimate as well, in its two aspects of natured and naturing. Metaphysical and religious ultimates typically go together. It would be strange, if not incoherent, to affirm as religiously ultimate something that is not thought to be metaphysically ultimate. The God of traditional Western religion, for example, is assumed to be the highest and most excellent form of being as well as the final source and sustainer of all that is. This means that God is held to be both metaphysically and religiously ultimate.

In Buddhism, by contrast, it is not the creator god Brahma who is regarded as either metaphysically or religiously ultimate, even if the existence of Brahma is conceded. Instead, the final truth and supreme reality behind all things is Nirvana—permanent, immovable, blissful, safe, and surpassingly good. Nirvana is what is metaphysically ultimate. For the Buddhist Nirvana is religiously ultimate as well: "the supreme goal and the one and only consummation of our life, the eternal, hidden, and incomprehensible Peace" (see Conze 1959: 39–40). In a naturalistic perspective nature is the root principle, power, or system from which all things spring and by which they are sustained. It is the final reality, the ultimate, all-encompassing context within which other realities have their being. And viewed religiously, it is unambiguously right or good. Nature is therefore entitled, in these respects, to be the focus of religious faith.

2. Nature is also the source of our existence as human beings. And it sustains us throughout our lives. It is the context upon which we crucially depend, not only as individuals but in our human histories, cultures, and societies. It has endowed us with all our human faculties and capacities: our social natures, our opposed thumbs, our big brains, our consciousness, our reason, our language, our freedom, our technological prowess, our artistic sensibility and creativity. We owe everything we are and have to nature. Should we not, therefore, reverence it and meditate upon its gifts with intense religious gratitude and fervor?

I attended a ballet concert a short time ago. I was deeply moved by the beauty of the performances, which featured stirring music by Brahms, Saint-Saëns, Rachmaninov, Schumann, and Ravel. The choreographer and dancers captured the spirit of the music in estimable degree, and I was struck by the graceful movements of the ballerinas and the soaring strength of the male dancers. The spectacle of the lithe movements of the human body against the background of the sonorous music was overwhelming. The music, the choreography, the orchestra, the performances all gave witness to the remarkable sensitivity and creativity of the human spirit. Humans are capable of dismal moral ugliness and evil, as we saw in the previous chapter. And we shall want to inquire further into the significance of this fact for a religion of nature in the next section. But humans are also capable of astoundingly beautiful aesthetic achievements, as illustrated by the splendor of these performances. There is something in us that not only responds to beauty but is also able to bring it into being—in such things as sculpture, painting, architecture, literature, but especially in music, which seems to resonate most closely with the deepest intimations and yearnings of the human heart. These artistic works and performances are achievements of natural beings, and they give expression to the aesthetic qualities and capacities endowed upon humans by nature. In celebrating the aesthetic sensibilities and accomplishments of humans we are also celebrating one significant aspect of the multiple marvels of nature.

These marvels, as reflected in the capabilities of human beings as creatures of nature, are worthy of religious gratitude, adoration, and praise. The capabilities have a dark and sinister side, as we saw. They can be expressed in violent, uncaring, ruthlessly destructive ways. But they are also capabilities for enormous moral good—for such things as protecting and nurturing one's family, educating the young, attending to the sick, counseling those who have lost their way, helping the needy and unfortunate, exhibiting courage and self-sacrifice in times of struggle and peril, drawing upon one's particular talents and strengths to contribute to the health and improvement of human society, and working with conscientious care for the integrity and flourishing of all the creatures of earth. There are countless doers of good in the world in all these areas, and this statement applies to institutions as well as individuals. Hospitals, schools, legal firms, government institutions, churches, synagogues, mosques, nonprofit charity organizations, and the like can and do accomplish much good. We should not allow our heartrending and honest acknowledgment of the deep entrenchments of moral evil in individuals and institutions to blind us to this fact or to reduce us to despair.

An example of the moral good that humans are capable of is the character and work of a woman in my Unitarian/Universalist church in Tallahassee, Florida. Her name is Norene Chase. Norene heads up the Sunday morning Forum in the church. She enlists people from within the church, from all over Tallahassee, and from elsewhere to speak in the Forum to members of the church—frequently about issues of social justice and environmental ethics. She is active in the League of Women Voters. She works with local environmental groups such as the Sierra Club and the Big Bend Environmental Forum. She has served as a vigorous member of the Green Sanctuary Committee and the Global Climate Change Action Committee in the church. She sells equal-exchange, fair-trade coffee. She recently participated in a five-mile walk to call attention to problems of pollution in local streams, rivers, and lakes. She works tirelessly with leaders of city and country government for social justice and on behalf of environmental causes. She circulates petitions and participates in political campaigns. Before her retirement, she was a nurse, ministering to the needs of the sick. With her husband Tom she raised a family as well. Now in her eighties, Norene continues to work with exemplary enthusiasm and commitment for the amelioration of human social evils and the welfare of nature as a whole. She sometimes gets discouraged by the amount of social evil and the extent of thoughtless despoliation of the natural environment, but she never stops working.

People like Norene inspire us with hope for the counterbalancing influences of moral goodness in a world that contains so much moral evil. This hope is bolstered when we bring to mind institutions across the world that have people like her in positions of leadership and are charged with her kind of moral compassion, energy, and vision. The policies of institutions of various types—governmental, financial, industrial, educational, ecclesiastical, and the like—can be influenced for the good, and sometimes decisively, by the patient, unflagging work of people of her character and devotion. This is especially true when like-minded people find ways to work together for social justice and the common good.

Moral evils are manifestations of one side of our freedom; moral goods are expressions of another. Without the freedom to do evil, there could not be the freedom to do good. The sources of moral evil are complex, and we are not all equally free in all situations or at all times. We can be victims of bad habits, addictions, abusive or neglectful upbringing, impoverished circumstances, corrupt institutions, unstable and unjust societies, and other bad influences of various kinds. Nevertheless, our capacity for moral goodness is a gift of nature to be cultivated and cherished, and to be set resolutely against evil institutions and the wantonly hateful deeds of humankind. Emphasis on maximum development of this capacity is a fundamental part of religion of nature, considered as both critic and ideal. Religious rightness and moral goodness do not come down to the same thing, but they are closely connected and each can contribute significantly to the other, as we shall see in a later chapter.

The gist of this second reason offered in defense of religion of nature, then, is that human beings, and all their capacities and accomplishments, lie within the scope of nature. They are not set apart from it but included within it. An important part of what we can honor and reverence in the majestic and mysterious powers of nature is the human species it has brought into being and the human lives, institutions, cultures, and histories for which it provides encompassing context and to which it gives continuing support. It is not that nature cares for us. Nature is not a conscious being. It is not quite right, therefore, to speak of it as indifferent. Not being a conscious being, it neither cares nor does not care. These are inappropriate terms to apply to it. But nature gave rise to us as a species as it did to all other species, and its finely coordinated processes continue to sustain us and to make our lives, achievements, hopes, and aspirations possible. Nature has also given us the gift of freedom, a freedom for which we must take responsibility and which we can use for good or ill. In these respects as in others, it is a proper focus of religious faith.

3. Nature is not something wholly outside us and beyond us, as is the case with many types of religious ultimate. It is within us, we are within it, and we are akin to it in all its aspects. We are material beings, as are all other beings within the natural order. We share DNA with other living creatures. We come into being and pass away, as all things natural do. We share with other creatures a common origin in evolutionary history. Like them, we are crucially dependent on our natural environment. We are also subject to its unforeseen or unforeseeable perils. We eat, we drink, we sleep, we seek shelter, we procreate, we endeavor to preserve and enhance our lives, just as they do. As Chang Tsai declares of himself in the epigraph to this chapter, each of us humans can declare: "even such a small thing as I finds an intimate place" in nature. What "directs the universe I regard as my nature. All people are my brothers and sisters, and all things are my companions."

We are at home here. This is where we belong, not in some realm beyond the earth or outside the constraints, contingencies, and capacities of the physical universe. The spatial images that pertain to a religion of nature are those of breadth and depth, not height. It is not to a transcendent, entirely different realm in the far reaches of the sky but to this familiar earth and our fellow creatures of earth that we look for solace and strength. Another Chinese thinker, Wang Fu-Chih, who developed Chang Tsai's metaphysics, has this to say about our place in the natural world:

> We humans . . . do not find the impersonal cosmic function cold, alien, or distant, although we know that it is, by and large, indifferent to and disinterested in our private thoughts and whims. Actually, we are an integral part of this function; we are ourselves the result of this moving power of *ch'i*. Like mountains and rivers, we are legitimate beings in this great transformation. (paraphrased by Tu Wei-Ming 1989: 73)

There is a deep sense of humility in this statement, but also a profound feeling of gratitude and wonder. It is appropriate for us to be here, but we should not overestimate our importance in the whole scheme of things. We are part of a vast system of nature that sustains us but is not focused exclusively or primarily on us.

Every aspect of nature, including us, is a manifestation of *ch'i*, the "vital force" of nature that can be identified with what we earlier called "nature naturing." This force produces, underlies, and maintains the distinctiveness and integrity of each thing that exists in the universe and the complex interconnections and interdependencies of these diverse things. It maintains them, however, not in static fixity or sameness, but in a dynamic, restless manner that—sometimes over eons of time but sometimes quite abruptly—gives rise to the new by transfiguring the old. Presumably, the human species as a whole will eventually be transfigured too, even as each member of it is now required to give up his or her place in nature at death in order that new members can come into being.

The focus of religious faith in religion of nature, therefore, is within us and around us. And what is within and around us gives testimony to nature's creative power that has given rise to all that is, sustains it in being, works continuously to refresh and renew it, and will eventually transform it into something radically new. Nature and its creative power are something close at hand, not something infinitely distant. They are something we can study with our science and thereby deepen and strengthen, rather than detract from, our religious understanding and commitment. We will never succeed in fathoming all or probably even most of nature's mysteries—especially the deep mystery of nature naturing—but we can make some progress in coming to understand them because nature suffuses our being and is part and parcel of what we are. We do not stop where nature begins, and nature does not stop where we begin. The distinction between us and other forms of life and orders of being is at most one of degree, not one of kind.

What all of this adds up to is that as we expand our comprehension of the depth and detail of nature's processes, we also expand our understanding of nature as the focus of religious faith. And we thereby expand our awareness of our place within the natural order, a place that demands our respect for all things natural and requires that we seek to live in balance with other natural beings. Nature is not distinct from the religious ultimate but identical with it. The two are not set in opposition, nor is one subordinate to the other. They are one and the same. Awareness of this fact, and for religion of nature it is the most fundamental fact of all, reorients our conventional conception of religion in the West, making its focus radically immanental and here-at-hand.

Not only that, but this change of focus gives the religious ultimate the utmost concreteness and embodiment. Religion of nature celebrates an incarnation of the ultimate that is unqualified and complete. It is not in its essential character pure spirit possessed of dubious omni-attributes set in radical contrast with everything else in the world, nor does its true mode of being lie in a diaphanous, faraway, impenetrably mysterious spiritual realm. We humans are made in this fully incarnate ultimate's image, but so is everything else in nature. From the tiniest grain of sand or most minute unicellular organism to the most sophisticated human being, everything is created *in imago naturae*. These closely related points—all calling attention to our intimate relation to nature and nature's intimate relation to us—constitute, I believe, a strong third reason in support of a religion of nature.

4. The fourth reason relates directly to the central issue of this book, the issue of good and evil. One of the main strengths of religion of nature

is that it does not have to struggle with the traditional theological problem of evil. It does not have to try to reconcile the alleged absolute goodness of God with the systemic natural and moral evils of the world. John Dupré states the point well:

> Philosophers and theologians have gone to great trouble through the ages to establish that the nature of the world is not wholly inconsistent with a benevolent creator (it's not really as bad as it looks; evil has distant good consequences we're not aware of; and so on). But the prospects for showing that the universe is so full of goodness that it could have been created only by a supremely benevolent being are about as unpromising as for any argument one could come up with. (Dupré 2003: 52)

For religion of nature, there is no conscious, purposive creator of the world. Therefore, there is no divine person to question about or to be held responsible for the presence of suffering and wickedness in the world. There is no God who needs to be hauled into the dock with urgent, highly pertinent questions in the way that Job sought to bring Yahweh to trial in the Hebrew Bible—in a lame attempt to find some convincing explanation for why Yahweh would permit such a horrendous amount of pain and misfortune to afflict innocent persons. In Job's case, Yahweh brushes his anxious interrogator aside with the response that there is such an enormous distance and difference between Yahweh and a puny mortal like Job that Job could never hope to understand Yahweh's reasons or purposes. So we are left with the seemingly intractable problem of why a God who is supposed to care so much seems to care so little.

Moreover, there is no need in a religion of nature to try to demonstrate the existence and character of a gracious, all-good God based upon our experiences of the world, a world exhibiting not only abundant goodness but a staggering amount of evil besides. According to religion of nature, the ambiguity of nature is a given, not a conundrum. Systemic natural evils are necessarily present in an orderly, law-like world where the regularities of nature can harm as well as help, depending on the circumstances. Were there no regularities, there could be no such thing as adaptation and survival. But failure to adapt is also failure to survive. A world in which change takes place and time is real is also a world in which some of the old must be left behind in order that new things and new possibilities can come into being. Creation and destruction work hand in hand. A world filled with diverse living beings is also going to be a world in which the demands of those beings will not always and in all circumstances be compatible, but will come into conflict and competition in the struggle for survival and enhancement of life.

Death is also a necessary part of life, given that the diversity of beings in the world would soon be choked by its spatial limits and finite physical resources were there no such thing as death. The good of freedom entails the possibility of misuses of freedom, and it entails a world orderly enough for the exercise of freedom to have predictable consequences for good or ill—consequences for which free beings can be held responsible. Systemic natural evils and moral evils do not pose unsolvable conceptual problems for religion of nature in the way that they tend to do for traditional versions of theism.

We are not pressed to square belief in a conscious, purposive, all-loving, all-powerful creator God with the pervasive ambiguities of the world. We still have to find ways to cope with evil, as people of all persuasions, religious or otherwise, have to do. But we are not tempted to deny the existence of evil, minimize its extent, explain it away, or dismiss it as a delusion based upon the limitations of our human purview, in order to keep intact belief in an absolutely good creator God. We can readily acknowledge and affirm the stubborn reality of evil and in that way do full justice to our experience. This is a distinct advantage of religion of nature and another reason for claiming nature as an appropriate focus for religious faith.

5. A fifth reason for placing our religious faith in nature is that the existence of nature does not have to be proved. Its existence seems obvious and undeniable, and it is tangible and real in a way that most putative religious ultimates are not. Evidence for the reality of nature lies ready at hand in all directions. There are different theories about the nature of nature, of course, and there are both philosophical and religious theories that deny the existence of nature outright. But the different theories about the nature of nature presuppose a nature to be theorized about, unless they regard nature itself as an illusion. And the philosophical or religious theories that do take nature to be something that is in the final analysis illusory—such as Absolute Idealism or Advaita Vedanta Hinduism—still have the formidable task of trying to show why the alleged illusion is so persistent and widespread, or why it should exist at all. They also have the task of explaining in what it is that the illusion lies, given their denial of the existence of anything other than the single absolute reality they allege. Acknowledging the existence of nature seems to be far less of an uphill battle. And proving with arguments the existence of a supernatural realm, or of a supernatural being or beings, even when one does acknowledge the reality of nature, is a daunting and generally unpersuasive undertaking, as the whole history of philosophies or religions devoted to this project clearly shows.

I do not wish to denigrate philosophical or religious positions that either deny the existence of nature outright or argue for the reality of something beyond and greater than nature. These positions deserve our attention and respect, and there is much that we can learn from them even if we come finally to disagree with their outlook. I only want to note the extraordinary difficulty of the conceptual tasks they set before us as compared with the relative ease with which we can accept the reality of nature and access it as an object of religious faith. This is not to say that a religion of nature is easy. It requires strong discipline and commitment, selfless dedication to the needs of others, and a lifetime of concentrated study, meditation, and practice. But I am saying that it is easier to grasp and to be convinced of conceptually than religions that deny the reality of nature or lay claim to the religious ultimacy of something outside of nature. And I am claiming this point as one of religion of nature's strengths.

6. Despite its being tangible and ready at hand in one sense, nature is no less awesome, mysterious, and wonderful than any other candidate for religious ultimacy. This is another point in its favor as the focus of religious faith. The sheer givenness of nature as we experience and conceive it today and as it continues to be transformed by the relentless workings of nature naturing, the creative-destructive forces that underlie it, is more than enough to dumbfound us. Nature is self-originating, self-renewing, self-transforming. How this is possible we cannot fathom, despite all our touted claims to intimate knowledge of natural processes. We work with what is given and the principles and powers it incorporates, but we cannot ultimately explain its presence. There is an incalculable complexity and intricacy of its processes before which we can only stand in amazement. Both its spatial extent—billions of galaxies, each with billions of stars stretching out into incredible distances—and its temporal extent—somewhere around fifteen billion years by current calculation—lie far beyond the limits of our puny imaginings. And we are only talking about one face of nature, brought into being by the mysterious power of nature naturing and eventually to be eroded away and replaced with a different face by that same power. What sorts of universe preceded this universe? What sorts will follow it? We have no way of knowing. All we can do is predict or retrodict on the basis of regularities and laws of the present universe in order to have some idea of its remote future or past. Even here, our speculations are fraught with uncertainty.

Then there is the incredible diversity of beings in this universe! The sweep of evolutionary history is something to be contemplated with wonder and awe. The millions of distinct species it has spawned boggle the mind. Some millions have been left by the wayside of evolutionary history as now extinct species. New ones are being created even as I write these words. Each species has its own distinctive way of life and its own peculiar place within nature as a whole. These species interact with and depend upon one another in complex ways, so complex that many of their mutual dependencies and modes of interaction remain unrecognized and unexplained. And each member of each species has its own outlook on the world, its own feeling or awareness, however murky or dim, of what the world is like and what it must take into account in order to survive. We may imagine something of what these outlooks might be like, but we can never do justice to them. We can never really enter into these creatures' worlds because we are incapable of living their lives. Their outlooks on the world remain ineluctably mysterious, as utterly mysterious at the end of the day as our own outlooks and projects would be to them.

We humans inhabit one part of a capacious earth with a plethora of interconnected processes, principles, and species upon which we crucially depend, and our earth, for all its grandeur and majesty, is a tiny particle in comparison with the enormity of the universe. What do we really know? How much do we really know? How much will we ever know? Very little, must be our honest answer. It is appropriate for us to take pride in the extent of our present knowledge so long as we are also willing to acknowledge the depth of our ignorance. The physicist David Bohm observed, for example, that matter possesses an infinity of properties, possibilities, and levels, and thus that no physical "law is absolute or final, but that each law provides a successively better approximation to an absolute truth that we can never possess in a finite time, because it is infinite in all of its aspects, both qualitative and quantitative" (1952 letter of Bohm quoted in Peat 1997: 140).

When we discuss metaphysical perspectivism in the next chapter, we will examine a principal way of coming to understand why so much of nature must remain awesome and impenetrably mysterious for human beings, no matter how far they may go in seeking to unlock its secrets. But there is also the point to be made that the farther humans do go in unlocking these secrets, the more amazing the intricacy and complexity of its processes become and the less likely we are to take them for granted. We have abundant evidence in support of this point with the progress made since the seventeenth century in scientific understanding of the processes of nature. We have only to contemplate what we now know of the workings of the human ear, eye, heart, brain, or the various cells of the human body to be dazzled by the wonders of nature. And this is to say nothing of the turbulent stochastic processes we have discovered to lurk beneath the surface of Isaac Newton's supposedly hard and indivisible atoms. I argued in a book published some time ago that one of the six essential functions of religious objects of all types is "hiddenness" (D. A. Crosby 1981: ch. 7). Nature exhibits inexhaustible hiddenness, and this fact constitutes one of its important qualifications as an appropriate focus of faith. There is more than enough mystery in nature to satisfy the most sensitive, awe-attuned, deeply wondering, and acutely responsive religious inquirers.

7. Finally, nature can be saving for those attuned to its presence and influence. It has the power to inspire, enhance, and renew our lives. We are natural beings in the deepest recesses of our bodies and spirits, and learning how to live in accordance with that fact provides us with both profound challenge and profound hope. We can be assured by the sense of being at home in nature, of belonging here with all the other creatures of earth. We can be grateful for the special powers nature has bestowed upon us and seek to use those powers in constructive, helpful ways. We

can learn how to accept and act upon our responsibilities as members of the household of earth.

Nature is saving in two respects: assurance and demand. The rejuvenation and transformation of life it bestows come with accompanying responsibilities. Let us first consider some of the responsibilities and demands that religion of nature imposes upon us. I speak here from personal conviction, and readers may disagree with some of what I shall say in this connection. But I hope that I shall at least gain a hearing and that the rationale for my position will be taken seriously. We should do all we can to refrain from inflicting needless harm on other human beings or on other natural beings of any kind. Hunting or fishing *for fun*, for example, would therefore seem to be seriously wrong in the perspective of religion of nature, just as inflicting such harm on other human beings would be. It is wrong because it uses animals and fish for our own gratification or pleasure and does not respect the right they have to be free of pain and to enjoy their lives as we seek to enjoy our own. There is predation enough in nature without our contributing to it as humans when we do not need to, and solely in the interest of so-called sport. Mistreating animals on factory farms is also flagrantly wrong. They have a right to live their lives in accordance with their natural needs and desires—the right to a free range, for example, as opposed to being cooped up in boxes or cages that give them scant space to move about, or as opposed to being crowded into filthy feed lots.

We should not experiment on animals except in cases where such experimentation is absolutely necessary to procure knowledge that can be used to help human beings and other animals as well with serious medical problems. We should not inflict pain and suffering on animals in searches for a better cosmetic, for example. Should we eat animals? We are omnivores by nature, but we do not need to eat meat to survive or even to thrive. Unlike other animals that are programmed by instinct to be predators, we have a choice in the matter in the circumstances of our present societies. Therefore, we do not have to add to the systemic natural evil of predation. We can do just as well with a proper diet of grains, vegetables, and vegetable products and probably gain better health by not eating such meats as pork and beef. It is also more efficient, on balance, to eat grains than to eat animals that have consumed the grains. And by not eating meat, we can also register our protest against the cruel treatment of animals in many agribusinesses today. We can also be cognizant of the water pollution in concentrated feedlots and the methane infused into the atmosphere that contributes to greenhouse gas and the problem of global warming.

Other ways in which the demand aspect of nature's saving message affects us is that we should refrain from needless or frivolous despoliation of the earth. If we do need for good reason to harm the earth, we should try in every way to restore it and not to leave it in a ruined state. This means such things as replanting trees, not cutting the tops off of mountains, not scarring the earth, not polluting the streams, not drilling for oil offshore or in wilderness areas, and not poisoning the atmosphere. We should avoid doing these things not only for our own sakes as human beings but for the sake of the earth itself, to reverence and preserve its integrity and natural state as much as is possible. In so doing, we enhance our attunement with the earth and our sensitivity to and respect for our natural home.

We should also work to conserve nonrewable sources of energy and to find renewable alternatives to them. We should recycle instead of just piling stuff up in our landfills. We should continue to set aside portions of land as wilderness and to keep these portions as pristine as possible in order that wildlife may flourish and that we may enjoy the delights of unspoiled nature. We should do all we can to avoid contributing to the extinction of rare species. Ecological ethics and environmental responsibility are integral parts of a religion of nature. Human social ethics is an essential part of it as well, and we shall have more to say about this topic later. In my view, human social ethics should be regarded as a subset of environmental ethics, for our obligation is to treat all living beings with respect and to reverence the earth as our natural home. We are not so much stewards of nature, presiding over it from without, as humble participants in nature who should do everything we can to keep our lives in balance with the rest of nature. Just as our technology gives us great power to inflict harm on nature, it also gives us great power to serve it in positive ways and to reverse the deleterious effects of our former neglect and mistreatment of our natural environment.

This is not a book on environmental ethics, and much more could obviously be said about this subject. I have only ventured a few general hints and suggestions about it. My point in doing so is to call attention to the kinds of *demand* implicit in a religion of nature. Responding to such demands can deepen our sense of connection with nature and make us more fully aware of what it means to be natural beings living in close relation to other natural beings, sharing their environments and contributing to or at least not interfering with their flourishing.

This feeling of connection and intimacy of relation is central to what is meant by the *assurance* aspect of nature as the focus of religious faith. We are not aliens in a strange land surrounded by strangers. We are not mere temporary visitors of earth. We are ourselves natural through and through, and therefore kin to all other natural beings. To attune ourselves with nature is to attune ourselves with the deepest levels of our being. We can rejoice in the privilege of being at home in this marvelous world.

My wife and I went to visit a friend named Anne Rudloe who lives by the seashore not far from our home in Northwest Florida. She had just had forty percent of her colon removed because of colon cancer. She would soon begin a series of chemotherapy treatments, and the outcome of these treatments was uncertain because the cancer had affected some of her lymph nodes. Our friend is a Zen Buddhist, and she commented that her present condition was to be the Olympics of her Buddhism, by which she meant the supreme test of the nurturing and sustaining power of her faith. We could tell that her faith was already meeting the test, because she was extremely calm in the face of her coming trial. She said with quiet assurance, "It's not all about our egos, and if people think it is, they are badly mistaken."

We walked out on the dock behind her home, and as we did so we caught sight of a gorgeous rainbow gracing the distant clouds over the blue waters of the bay. That rainbow was a kind of epiphany for me. It was a sign of hope for her recovery, which my wife and I yearned for, but it was also a sign that whatever happens, all is ultimately well. Our friend's Buddhism is predicated on the idea of no-self, the conviction that there is no permanent substantial self underlying the changing circumstances of our lives but only a series of interconnected experiences. This stream of experience will someday be interrupted and brought to a close by our deaths, however those deaths may occur. We have no reason to think that we will live forever as the individuals we now are, and we certainly should not put all of our religious eggs in the basket of that hope—a recipe for anxious self-centeredness that is for me, as for our friend, the antithesis of genuine religious faith and commitment.

Our deaths are not a good from our own perspectives, and especially not from the perspective of those who love us and will mourn our passing. Some deaths are preceded by profound suffering and pain, and not all deaths take place in the fullness of time. But religion of nature encourages us to come to terms with the inevitability and finality of death as part of the system of nature as a whole. As a combination of evil and good, death bears testimony to the ambiguity of nature. It is an ambiguity without which, as we have seen, many of the goods we hold most dear—including the good of the evolution and continuing existence of human life—could not exist.

It is enough, then, that we live for a time and finally become reabsorbed into the larger whole from which we came. New persons with new hopes and dreams, new challenges and trials, will come into being after us, even as such persons preceded our births. This is the way of nature, and with it we can rest content. The permanence of nature itself in its various evolving forms contrasts with the impermanence of our lives and of all the particular constituents of nature. Change is the name of the game, so far as any particular thing is concerned, and as particular persons we are integral parts of that game. In the perspective of religion of nature, no human person can be expected to live forever, either here on earth or elsewhere. To live is also eventually to die, a truth that applies without exception to all the creatures of earth. In this respect we share in the character and fate of all those other creatures. The assurance dimension of a saving faith in nature is, in large measure, learning to accept this fact and to surmount an obsessive preoccupation with ourselves and our survival as individuals by focusing on what both our lives and our deaths can contribute to the whole scheme of things. This outlook is closely akin to that of my wife's and my Buddhist friend, and it is the outlook I endorse and recommend as a proponent of a religion of nature.

We can be assured that our lives amount to something and are worthwhile, even as we acknowledge that they must eventually end in our deaths. While we live, we can devote ourselves to one another and to the whole system of nature, and in that life of devotion we can find assurance, confidence, and peace. We can be inspired and renewed by the beauties and wonders of nature as we live our lives, opening ourselves to those beauties and wonders in every way we can. We can also be receptive to the salutary possibilities of events over which we have no control or ability to predict but which can sometimes give unanticipated depth and meaning to our lives. Such events can be regarded as events of grace, transformative gifts which we can humbly accept and for which we can give hearty thanks. We can prepare our souls for the evils that can befall us as finite beings subject to the powerful forces of nature or as members of a human society that includes the scourge of evildoers and our own susceptibility to immoral deeds or to passive complicity in society's evils. We can fight against moral evils and seek ways to protect ourselves and other parts of nature against nature's systemic natural evils. All of these responses are parts of the saving potential of nature as the focus of religious faith.

Nature's power to rejuvenate and inspire is not easy to put into words. All of us experience it at various times in our lives, and some more frequently than others. It is not just something that occurs to us at random, although it is sometimes like that. We can prepare ourselves for the redemptive powers of nature through spiritual meditation and practice, and we can do so in the company of others, not just in times of solitude. In closing this section of the chapter, I want to meditate for a moment on these questions: Why do we feel refreshed and renewed by being outside—in the woods, by the seashore, atop a mountain, in a field of wildflowers, or observing the behavior of wild animals? Just what is it that we experience and feel? And how do this experience and feeling compare with being in the presence of human artifacts and artificial human surroundings?

One possible answer is that the human artifacts and surroundings are typically static finished products, while nature is always changing, always in progress. The daytime sky, for example, is a kaleidoscope of varying types of cloud moving swiftly or floating serenely across a background of such varying shades as blue, violet, red, pink, orange, or grey. Each new surging ocean wave is different from the preceding one, while the overall pattern of the waves can change dramatically from one day to the next. As mountain hikers are well aware, mountain vistas and weather are far from being forever the same. They can change in the twinkling of an eye, and the mountaineer needs to be prepared for such abrupt changes. There is also the cycle of the seasons and the rhythm of day and night, as well as the wheeling circuits of the planets and stars. The vitality and activity of nonhuman nature chimes in with our own vitality and activity as living beings. Human artifacts and surroundings, by contrast, are typically inert, passive, finished, and unresponsive.

Another answer to the question of why we find refreshment and inspiration in being outside and away from our cities and towns is that we are removed—if only for a brief time—from the clamor and hubbub of our life in human society, a life that is typically suffused if not overwhelmed by features of the human built environment, by human duties and routines, by human discourse and communication, by habitual human-centered patterns of thought, by human projects, problems, and concerns. In the outdoor world of fields, forests, mountains, deserts, and seas, amid creatures of the wild, we can be jolted into awareness that we are a small but still significant part of the magnificence of nature as a whole and that our cultures, technologies, and societies are grounded in and deeply dependent upon the environing world. The distraction and din of everyday existence in human society can be muted for a time, and we can be made acutely sensitive to the quieter, more serene presences and rhythms of the nonhuman natural world. These presences and rhythms can bring peace and rest to the soul.

There is a sense, then, in which nonhuman nature is a deep calling unto deep, evoking responses from the depths of our being. I think we all at some level understand emotionally and experientially what I am trying to say, difficult though it is to give it explicit articulation. Perhaps the poets, and especially the nature poets, are best at giving it linguistic expression. It can also be brought home to us in sometimes startlingly powerful ways by the mysterious powers of music, painting, and the other arts. The prose writer Marjorie Kinnan Rawlings does an exquisite job of describing the healing awareness of being an intimate part of the whole of nature as she speaks of a mood that swept over her during a visit to a lakeside hammock near her home in the heart of Florida:

> The jungle hammock breathed. Life went through the moss-hung forest, the swamp, the cypresses, through the wild sow and her young, through me, in its continuous chain. We were all one with the silent pulsing. This was the thing that was important, the cycle of life, with birth and death merging one into the other in an imperceptible twilight and an insubstantial dawn. The universe breathed, and the world inside it breathed the same breath. This was the cosmic life, with suns and moons to make it lovely. It was important only to keep close enough to the pulse to feel its rhythm, to be comforted by its steadiness, to know that Life is vital, and one's own living a torn fragment of a larger cloth. (Rawlings 1942: 39)

The wonder of the cycles of nature and the majesty, splendor, and beauty of all of nature's ever-changing processes and interconnected patterns can thrill the heart and stir the soul. The bustling activity of earth's amazingly diverse creatures—each busily pursuing its own distinctive projects and tasks—can add a special kind of fascination and gladness to our days.

Another Floridian, Zen Buddhist practitioner and professional biologist Anne Rudloe (the personal friend I talked about earlier), describes a sudden, overwhelming experience of what it means to be at home in nature in a chapter of her book *Butterflies on a Sea Wind*. The chapter is appropriately entitled "Forest Zen," and in it she paints this scene:

> As I sat against the pine tree, with frogs, crickets, and the wind in full hullabaloo, a sudden awareness of continuity, and the self-arising organic nature of reality, arose. It was four-dimensional, extending through time as well as space. Tree and insect, foraging bird and the sitter on a log, and the bracket fungus on the log, we all were a piece of the same living fabric, just as were all the past lineages of primates in my ancestry and all the ancestors of the bracket fungus. For every relationship of which I was aware, there were at least a thousand more I hadn't seen. (Rudloe 2002: 129)

Such experiences are part of the assurance side of the saving powers of nature. They bring to heart and mind what we are: children of nature and members of the far-flung family of all of nature's creatures. Nature's saving power, in the form of both its demands and its assurances, is the seventh and final reason I am adducing in support of its fitness as the focus of religious faith.

THE WHOLE OF NATURE AS SACRED

Some religious naturalists respond to the ambiguity of nature or its admixtures of goods and evils by arguing that it is not the whole of nature that is deserving of religious faith but only a part of nature. We should focus, they insist, only on those aspects of nature that are creative and constructive, and that express or produce unequivocal goodness. It is these aspects alone that are sacred and holy, or that qualify for the designation of what I have called religious rightness. The dark and sinister side of nature, consisting of what I have termed its systemic natural evils and the moral evils of its human creatures, should be rejected forthrightly as candidates for inclusion in the scope of religious commitment.

The twentieth-century religious naturalist Henry Nelson Wieman is an example of this approach. The term he uses for what he deems to be the appropriate object of religious commitment is the traditional term *God*. Wieman's God is not a supernatural being or person but an impersonal process. God is entirely immanent within nature but is only a part of nature, not the whole of nature. Moreover, God for Wieman "is not the creator, meaning the mysterious source of everything. God is only the source of the good" in everything (Wieman and Horton 1938: 267). In a work written several years later than the one just quoted, Wieman has an even more restrictive conception of God; there he identifies God as the source of *human* good (Wieman 1946).

Wieman's colleague for a time at the University of Chicago Divinity School, Bernard Loomer, took a position toward the end of his career on the nature of God (while teaching at the Graduate Theological Union in Berkeley, California) that stands in sharp contrast with that of Wieman. According to Loomer, God or the appropriate focus of religious faith is the totality of the world. This totality is for him undeniably ambiguous. It contains such things as order and disorder, creation and destruction, pleasure and pain, good and evil. A God identified with only one side of such oppositions would lack adequate "size" to be God. Such a God would be hopelessly small, limited, and abstract, in contrast with the vastness, complexity, and concreteness of the dynamic world of our experience. An important implication of Loomer's position is that an adequate religious object must not be centered mainly or exclusively on human beings and their problems and concerns but must encompass the whole of nature. Because the world exhibits the ambiguity of the oppositions just mentioned and those to which we are calling attention in this book, Loomer concludes that God must also be regarded as ambiguous. "[A]n ambiguous God," he asserts, "is of greater stature than an unambiguous deity" (Loomer 1987: 43). This ambiguous God of which he speaks is none other than the whole of nature, a nature he views as "holy ground" that "contains and yet enshrouds the ultimate mystery inherent within existence itself" (Loomer 1987: 42). The view I am taking in this book in arguing for a religion of nature is close to Loomer's view in the respects mentioned here, but I see no reason to refer to nature as God. For me, nature is sacred but not divine.

Let us now consider some reasons for concluding, with Loomer, that an adequate focus of religious commitment must be ambiguous. Some of these reasons have been presented or adumbrated earlier, but we can now summarize them and with this summary bring this chapter to a close. The first reason is that nature's goods and evils, both systemic and moral, go necessarily together. The one cannot be had without the other because the two are intimately connected and correlated, as we have already seen. It is artificial and abstract in the extreme to think otherwise. The second reason is that a view such as Wieman's makes the religious object out to be something less than metaphysically ultimate. The religious ultimate for him is only a part of nature, the nature that he admits to be metaphysically ultimate.

A virtue of Loomer's position and my own is that it keeps the two types of ultimacy together, a view that, to me, makes more religious and philosophical sense. As I noted earlier, one of the things that entitles nature to be a viable candidate for religious ultimacy is its metaphysical ultimacy. And if we include all of the features, manifestations, and powers of nature and not just those that are constructive and good in the purview of what we affirm as religiously ultimate, then we must affirm a nature that is radically ambiguous. A difference between my position and Loomer's is that Loomer's position can be regarded as a kind of pantheism, but mine is not. My position is not a kind of pantheism because I do not call nature "God" and thus do not regard the whole of nature as divine in the way that Loomer and other pantheists, such as Benedict Spinoza, do. I concur with Loomer, however, in viewing nature as sacred or as "holy ground." The sacred or holy is that which we reverence as the focus of religious faith and that which deserves to be so reverenced. I have given reasons so far in this book and will continue to do so for responding to nature in this way.

Third, Wieman's position, especially in his book *The Source of Human Good*, gravitates too far in the direction of anthropocentrism. It focuses too much on what is good for humanity and not enough on what is good throughout nature as a whole. He tends to regard as religiously right only those aspects of nature that conduce to human well-being. By contrast, Loomer and I find religious rightness in the whole of nature and thus avoid the kind of humanism or anthropocentrism toward which Wieman's outlook, especially in his later writings, steers (see Shaw 1995: 66, 69–70 and *passim*). In finding this rightness in nature as a whole, however, Loomer and I must affirm nature's ambiguities as the price to be paid for its goods, and we must cease to center our religious faith exclusively or even primarily on human beings. Humans have their place in the holy ground that is nature as a whole, but they are one type of living being among others, all of whom—especially in light of the ecological consciousness that has come to the fore in recent years—must be understood to be critical to one another's existence and to be richly deserving of being included within the scope of religious commitment and concern.

In the fourth place, I think that a position such as Wieman's tends strongly to confuse the religious meaning of "good" with its moral meaning. Affirming the religious rightness or goodness of nature as a whole does not mean that we have to compromise in any way the importance of moral goodness or of striving for it in all possible ways. We should not expect to derive our moral standards and practices from nature in some kind of slavish or mechanical way. Nature provides a context for moral delibera-tion and the construction of moral principles, but it does not give us those principles. As free beings with the gifts of language, reason, and reflective experience, we must develop those principles on our own and in light of our shared historical experiences.

It is certainly important that we do so, and doing so can be a signifi-cant part of what it means to practice a religion of nature. But it does not require that nature be unambiguously good in a moral sense of that term. I believe that Wieman wanted to affirm only a part of nature as appropriate for religious commitment and concern because he assumed that the religious ultimate must be morally good or a moral guide for human life, and that it must be so in an unambiguous way. It is true that he warned us against being too complacent about our past or current moral accomplishments or existing moral standards and that he believed that his type of religious faith could inspire and motivate us toward higher goods—even at the expense of destroying some of the older ones. But his focus tended to be too exclusively humanistic and moral, and that is perhaps the main reason why he could have no truck with nature's ambiguities. We will return in a later chapter of this book to address in more detail the issue of the relations between moral goodness and the distinctively religious sense of goodness and value—what I call religious "rightness."

The fifth and final reason for affirming the whole of nature as religiously ultimate, and for not acquiescing in Wieman's notion that only a part of it is to be seen as ultimate, is that I am convinced of the need for a thoroughgoing perspectivist conception of nature that makes it impossible to draw the kinds of clean, unambiguous lines between good and evil that Wieman's position seems to presuppose. Presentation of this conception of nature is the subject of the next chapter, and it will be developed and defended there. Suffice it to say here that it calls seriously into question a central part of Wieman's outlook on nature and his concept of the focus of religious faith.

Before taking leave of this chapter, I want to respond to an objection to it that I think is fundamental and far-reaching. The objection is that I have no business proclaiming the rightness of nature or its fitness as a focus of religious faith because I have not experienced the kinds of devastating evils, either systemic natural or moral, or both, that some people have in the present and throughout history. I have no right to speak for them from the vantage point of my rather cloistered and sheltered middle-class life, with the kind of physical and mental health I presently enjoy, my relatively solid and secure upbringing, the good fortune of my extended education and academic career, and my citizenship in the relative peace and security of the United States in the twenty-first century. Moreover, I have not lost loved ones except in the fullness of time, and I have not experienced the ravages of the kinds of natural disaster I described earlier in this book. It is easy for you, the objector might say, to proclaim nature's religious rightness and goodness despite its ambiguities. But if called upon to suffer as some have suffered, you might well change your mind!

I deeply respect this objection. And it is perfectly true that I might at some future point in my life and thought change my outlook on nature and human life. I very much want to be open to the kind of counterevidence the objector cites, or to any kind of counterevidence that I might later discover to be relevant. And I do want to hear the fullest possible elaboration of the objector's outlook on the world, because it is highly germane to what is being claimed here. But I also want to remind the objector and the reader that a central claim of this book is that nature is radically ambiguous and that we must take this ambiguity fully into account in our religious outlook and life. Part of the ambiguity is that nature's systemic and moral goods and evils do not affect every one of us in the same ways or to the same degree. And some of these can be horrible and perhaps even unbearable.

If we are among the fortunate, as assuredly I am, we can give thanks for that fact. But we should not do so without a deep feeling of sadness and compassion for all the people and other kinds of creature in this world who are not so fortunate. We should allow them to speak for themselves, as I am seeking to do here. None of us can entirely escape the particularities of our perspectives. And we should regard the gift of a reasonably settled and happy life as a charge and responsibility to use the resources of that life in service of others, especially those others who are not as fortunate as we might be. One of the ways in which I am trying to do this is my writing of this book. I want us all to be honest about what we are up against and not to be led down the garden path of a less than relentlessly honest religious view. If there is no such thing as a wholly unambiguous "sweet by-and-by" or a God untouched by the ambiguities of the world, as I have argued, then we must make do with what we have. It is all we can do and the best we can do. The love of nature as religiously ultimate—and it can be a joyful and grateful love—must be accompanied by a frank, full, and humble awareness of its potential and actual evils.

FOUR

PERSPECTIVISM, PLURALISM,
AND AMBIGUITY

━━━━━━━━━━━━━━━━━━━━━━━━━━━━━

There is no possible point of view from which the world can appear as
a single fact.

—William James, *Essays on Faith and Morals*

In this chapter I want to defend a version of metaphysical perspectivism and
to show how it relates to a pluralistic vision of reality, on the one hand, and
a pluralistic approach to truth and value, on the other. These positions in
their turn entail that reality is radically ambiguous and that our notions of it
must take this ambiguity fully into account—a conclusion that applies with
equal force to any plausible conception of a reality that contains distinct
entities. The ambiguity of nature that is a central concern of this book
follows from the perspectivist interpretation of reality I shall defend here.
For perspectivists, there is no alternative to or escape from ambiguity, and
the ambiguity of nature should not be considered a conceptual barrier to its
being the focus of religious faith. The problem remains, of course, of how
to respond to nature's ambiguities and how to find confidence and meaning
for the living of our lives in the face of the evils of nature. I shall continue
to have more to say about this problem as our discussion proceeds.

METAPHYSICAL PERSPECTIVISM

What is metaphysical perspectivism? It can be succinctly defined as the
view that everything that exists in the world is a distinctive perspective
on everything else. Perspectives of humans and other sentient beings are
included in this statement, but it is not restricted to them. All the elemental
particles, atoms, molecules, compounds, inorganic and organic entities and

combinations of these entities, including human beings and their histories, cultures, and societies, and all of the actions, reactions, functions, qualities, and traits of these particular things and their relations are included. No two perspectives or systems of them are exactly alike. Each of their constituents is distinctive in some degree and occupies a unique perspective in comparison with the rest. So I am not talking here about just a subjectivist or episte-mological version of perspectivism, namely, that the world is perspectival merely from the standpoints of human beings, but about a grander, more inclusive—explicitly metaphysical—perspectival character of everything that exists. Perspectivism is a fact about the world and everything in the world, not just a fact about human interpreters of the world, although the character, outlooks, and experiences of humans are included within that larger perspectivism.

Friedrich Nietzsche was a notable perspectivist of the nineteenth century, and the following statement from his posthumously collected notes published under the title *The Will to Power* shows that his version of per-spectivism applies to everything without exception, as does mine:

> [T]he world, apart from our condition of living in it, the world that we have not reduced to our being, our logic and psychologi-cal prejudices, does not exist as a world "in itself"; it is essentially a world of relationships; under certain conditions it has a differing aspect from every point; its being is essentially different from every point, every point resists it—and the sum of these is in every case quite incongruent. (Nietzsche 1968: 568)

There are several things I want to call attention to in this statement. The first is that there is no such thing as an "in-itself" world apart from or inde-pendent of all perspectives. To be is to be the constituent of a perspective, and all and only such constituents make up the world. The second thing is that to be is to be in relation. There are no isolated, entirely self-suffi-cient beings of any kind. What a thing is or becomes depends crucially on its contexts of relation. It is what it is as informed and affected by those contexts and would not be the same in other contexts. As Ronald Preston Phipps notes, "The concrete and particular cannot be comprehended apart from the broader realities from which they arise, within which they exist and interact, and to which they causally contribute" (Phipps 2005: 177).

Nevertheless, and this is the third thing, each being has a character and integrity of its own and thus its own distinctive perspective on the world within its contexts—a perspective unique to itself that cannot be duplicated in its entirety by any other thing in the world. Hence, there is an irreducible incongruity among perspectives. They cannot be summed up within or made completely compatible with any other perspective, no matter how inclusive or all-comprehending that other perspective might be claimed to be.

Even if there were such a thing as a God, for example, God's perspective would have to be different in some important respects from those things in the universe that are not God, just as their perspectives would have to be different in some important respects from God's. This is obviously true if God is conceived of as infinite and the world's entities as finite. Something infinite could no more have complete comprehension of what it is like to be finite than something finite could be expected to comprehend completely what it is like to be infinite. Even a finite God would, by virtue of being God, have a different perspective on the world than would beings other than itself, and could not enter completely into those other perspectives. It is impossible for God to know the world exhaustively or to do full justice from God's perspective to all that is in the world. There is no in-itself world, then, from God's standpoint or from any other standpoint. The world is perspectival through and through. Any approach to it is bound to be partial, even though there are different degrees of such partiality, and there can be no smooth summing up of all the actual or possible approaches to the world.

Just what is the world? In this book I am arguing that there is nothing beyond the world of nature. Nature is all the reality there is. What, then, is nature? Nature is no single thing but a multifarious complex of countless different things and the interrelated, but also finally contrasting, perspectives of those things. Religion of nature differs from traditional monotheism in many respects, but an important one is implied here. The object of faith and commitment in religion of nature is not a God assumed to be forever the same, absolutely one, or serenely all-comprehending, but nature regarded as a volatile, many-faceted intermixture of continuity and change, unity and diversity, and perspectives upon perspectives—no single perspective of which can be thought to comprehend, encompass, or contain the totality of all other perspectives. Even the idea of a *totality* of perspectives is a contradiction because of its suggestion that perspectives, despite their varying degrees of incommensurability, could be summed up into some kind of final unity.

This being the case, religion of nature can also rightly be called "religion of natures." I avoid the latter term because it is stylistically awkward, but it does have the virtue of calling attention to the close affinity between a perspectivist and a pluralistic metaphysics. In fact, the first, as I view it, clearly entails the second. Precisely because of the perspectivist metaphysical outlook I am arguing for here, nature must be understood to be an intricate combination of the one and the many—smooth threads of commonality, connection, and unity weaving only partially together rough, resistant, and still dangling strings of ineliminable diversity. Associations or predilections that might cause religion of nature's view of nature to be misinterpreted along monotheistic lines as a fixed and final unity rather than recognizing it as a dynamic, complex, variegated system involving aspects of both unity and plurality need to be made explicit and left behind. While it is true that nature is the *single object of religious commitment* for proponents of religion of nature, it is by no means to be thought of as unqualifiedly single, simple, or unitary in its own right. If I were called upon for a concise definition of what I take the term *nature* to mean, I would say something like the following: Nature is a system (or complex of systems) of countless things and sorts of things that work together in a generally orderly and predictable fashion but that also exhibit aspects of stubborn distinctiveness, diversity, and individuality, as well as of ongoing spontaneity, innovation, and change.[1]

Perspectivism can also be termed "relationalism." For instance, whatever world there is for us humans—or, more properly, *worlds there are*, since each person's perspective on the world is bound to be different in important respects from every other person's—is a world or worlds in relation to our general perspective as human beings. If we had ten senses instead of only five, the world for us would not only be quite different but perhaps unimaginably different. Without highly developed cultures and languages, our lived world would be altered in ways it is hard now to conceive. We have no way of knowing precisely or even to high degrees of approximation what it would be like to be an intestinal bacterium, aphid, mosquito, bumblebee, ant, aardvark, duck-billed platypus, blue whale, or osprey—and routinely to experience and respond to the world from any one of these diverse perspectives.

There is thus one respect in which the world is other than us, but another in which it is contained within us. The world is the perceptible, measurable, detectable, expressible world about which we are or can become aware. This is the only world fully meaningful to us or accessible to us. We may be able to some extent to enter empathetically and imaginatively into some aspects of the world as seen from the perspectives of other creatures, but we can never capture in all its fullness and concreteness exactly what it is like to be such creatures or to occupy their perspectives on the world. The world for them is not the same thing as the world for us. We will always be limited to viewing their perspectives only as aspects of those perspectives that can be envisioned or extrapolated from within our own perspectives as human beings.

The world and each and every aspect of it are neither completely external nor internal. They are relational. In our case as human beings, our instruments and theories, and such things as the acquisition of other languages and learning about other cultures, may augment or alter our perspectives in various ways, but they cannot eliminate the limited standpoints and angles of vision of our experiences, conceptualizations, and understandings, or the relational, perspectival character of what the world is and must forever be for us.

This analysis applies to any two human beings, no matter how much they may share the same background and culture and no matter how close they may be or become to each other. My experiences, memories, expectations, outlooks, interests, and capabilities are different in significant degrees from any one else's. Do we all live in the same world, then? We share a world to the extent that our perspectives overlap; our worlds are different to the extent that they do not. The ratio of similarities and differences in two persons' outlooks and experiences can change over time as they get to know one another better. But the differences can never be completely eradicated; they may even be enhanced as the persons grow closer together and in consequence discover more differences in their respective selves.

We should not expect the differences to be eliminated, nor would we want them to be. It is just this combination of similarity and difference that enables us to interact and communicate with one another, but that also enables each of us to be a unique self. It would be a boring world if other persons were nothing more than replicas of one another. Since in that event none of us would have anything unique or distinctively our own to offer the world, our existence would make little difference to the world, and it would be hard to see how we could even matter to ourselves. So our uniqueness as persons is vitally important, but it is always developed and expressed in relation to a world that is multidimensional and replete with perspectives other than our own.

What I have just noted about humans and their relations to one another and to an inherently relational world applies to other creatures, entities, systems, and situations of every kind. My world and my cat's world, for example, are not the same, despite their many overlaps. I do not share her fascination with cockroaches, for example, and she does not share my fascination with books. But we both need food, water, and shelter. And we both enjoy each other's company. The world of a feline in the wild is notably different from our two worlds, even though that feline too requires food, water, and shelter to survive. Each is a perspective or set of perspectives upon other perspectives and sets of perspectives. These perspectives relate to one another, intersect with one another, and respond to one another but also retain the distinctiveness and incommensurability of their own unique points of view. Similarly, inorganic entities and systems of such entities exert their energy and produce their effects upon the world from their own distinctive perspectives, and they are affected, in turn, by the energy and effects of other entities and systems of entities.

Being is always and only being in relation, just as truth is always and only truth in relation. The same can be said of value. There is no such thing as completely external being, truth, or value existing outside all contexts of interpretation, on the one hand, nor, on the other, should these things be conceived as constituted in their entirety by an internal perspective or set of perspectives. Thus, we are not entitled to think of nature as an in-itself world, shorn of perspectival constraints or relations, nor to conceive of it as the whole-cloth construction or creation of any given internal perspective or set of perspectives. Being, truth, and value are outcomes of the relations between what is internal to a perspective and what is external to it. But what is external to it is also perspectival in its own character. Perspectives can partially intersect and relate to one another, but they are also conditioned and constrained by one another.

My claims to being, truth, or value are elicited or constrained by ob-duracies of the world—that is, by other perspectives and influences external to myself—but it is a world as experienced and viewed from my perspec-tive, though not wholly constituted by it. There is no such thing as total objectivity, but there is also no such thing as total subjectivity. There are neither pure things-in-themselves nor pure subjects-in-themselves. What there is—what we and the world external to ourselves are made up of—is pervasive complexes of perspectivity and relationality.

Does reality sink into a morass of relativity, then? Is there no such thing as a wholly objective nature, a nature independent of the diverse perspectives upon it? My answer to these questions is that we should think of reality as an intricate web of relations rather than as a bottomless morass of relativity. Objective nature is construed in a perspectivist metaphysics as combining the complex interrelationships and the irreducible diversities of perspectives. These interrelations and diversities are objectively real, and they transcend any given perspective or collection of perspectives. Were there no distinctive perspectives, there would be no such thing as nature, but it is also true that were there no interactions or interrelations of perspec-tives, there would be no such thing as nature. Each perspective acts upon others and is acted upon by others. It experiences what is "there" from its own "here." Not only is it influenced and affected by what is there, it also exerts its own influence upon or places its own interpretation upon what is there. The reality lies, therefore, in this interrelation of inner and outer, the perspectives and what they are perspectives upon. It is perspectives and systems of perspectives all the way down and all the way up.

Moreover, this is not a static complex of interrelationships but a dy-namic one, as diverse entities and their distinctive perspectives enter into new contexts of relationship and explore or are affected by new and differ-ent aspects of a perspectival world. Entities and their respective perspectives are also constantly coming into being and passing away. The essential point about this perspectival world is that no single perspective can ever hope to explore, affect, be affected by, or relate to every aspect of the world. The distinctiveness and diversity of perspectives, their unique combination both of capacities and limitations, prohibits any such thing as a complete comprehension or inclusion of all the perspectives, possible or actual, that lie outside of any single perspective or particular combination of perspectives.

JUDGMENTS OF TRUTH AND VALUE

We should not conclude from these statements that all perspectives are equally adequate when it comes to judgments of truth or value. Some perspectives are more inclusive than others. That is, some capture more truth or value than others. Some perspectives are false, misinformed, or misleading in ways that others are not. Some fail to be sufficiently responsive to possibilities of value. And some can be perniciously evil, as we saw when we talked about evildoers in the world. I am not proposing a complete relativity of perspectives when it comes to truth and value. But I am denying the possibility of *absolute* truths or *absolute* values, just as I am denying the possibility of absolute being, whatever that might be taken to mean. Alleged absolutes of any kind violate the principles of perspectivity and relationality.

The epistemological or valuative perspectives of today might be called into question by the perspectives of the future, for example, as new insights, theories, or experiences come into view. We have no way of knowing with absolute certainty that this will not be the case. Or one perspective might be called into question by another perspective not yet met or dealt with. It will always be the case, moreover, that truth and value relate to and are conditioned by some context or other, some specific standpoint or orientation. Contexts, standpoints, and orientations may change over time and change in unexpected ways.

Certainty as a psychological state at a given time is no guarantee of epistemic certainty or absolute value. Past certainties have regularly given way to different outlooks in the present, as history so clearly shows, and present outlooks may have to yield to different outlooks of the future. The conviction that the orbits of the planets are and *must* be circular (rather than elliptical) was taken for granted for many centuries, for example, before it was countered by the astronomical observations and theories of a more recent time. And the institution of slavery had a long and generally unquestioned status prior to the period of the Enlightenment, with its insistence on personal freedom as an inalienable right of all human beings.

In any event, relatively high degrees of probability at a given time are sufficient. Absolutes are not required for warranted claims to knowledge or dependable value commitments. Nor is there need for such claims or commitments to be derived from absolutes. There is a middle ground between absolute truths and values, on the one hand, and completely relative ones, on the other. Perspectivism does not question the need to weigh crucial differences of degree in the status of particular claims to truth and value. In fact, it renders these claims more responsible by insisting that they be seen as probabilistic at best, rather than absolute, and therefore as needing always to be receptive to possible new ways of thinking and new kinds of evidence wherever these may be found. A perspectivist view of knowledge and value seeks by its very nature for inclusion of or consideration of as many relevant perspectives as possible. Not all other perspectives are relevant to a given perspective, and some perspectives may be incompatible with it. But those that are relevant and those that are at least partially compatible may provide from their different angles of vision enrichment of the original perspective and compensation for what may be lacking in it. So it is important that the latter be open to what can be learned from the former. Different perspectives can be complementary and offer access to complementary truths and values despite their lack of total commensurability with one another.

Let me sum up what has been said so far in this chapter. The idea that the world is made up of diverse perspectives and constituents of perspectives, and that each of the perspectives has elements of incongruity, however large or small, with other perspectives, implies a pluralistic, multifarious world, a world combining order and disorder, similarity and difference, cooperation and conflict, integration and separation. It is a world whose stubborn multiplicity and diversity cannot be resolved from any perspective or set of perspectives into complete oneness or unity, in spite of the fact that it contains an impressive amount of coherence and interrelatedness.

This perspectivist metaphysics also implies a pluralistic (but not relativistic) outlook on truth and value, meaning that no assumption or assertion about truth or value can be judged to be absolute. Every such assumption or assertion reflects the limitations and conditions of a particular perspective as it relates to other perspectives. Such claims are also shown to be provisional by the fact that they are susceptible to modification or abandonment in light of the perspectives of a later time no matter how certain they may seem to be at a given time. Finally, a more adequate or inclusive account of truth or value may require reference to other perspectives that are partially incommensurable with the perspective from which a particular account is presented or assumed. The differences between two or more perspectives can be as instructive as the respects in which they concur. It is important to take into account not only overlaps of perspectives but also ways in which they do not coincide. Particular perspectives may complement one another in important respects despite their differences, and each may be broadened and enriched by encounter with the other.

PERSPECTIVISM AND AMBIGUITY

The perspectivist vision of being, truth, and value dovetails with the concept of nature developed earlier, namely, the concept of it as radically ambiguous and necessarily so. As we have seen, nature is neither unqualifiedly good nor is it unqualifiedly evil. It is a necessary blend of good and evil because many of its goods are made possible only because of the possibility of its evils. We have also noted that no plausible conception of a religious ultimate can save it from ambiguity, so long as it has any connection with a world distinct from itself, a world possessing any significant degree of autonomy or independence. For God to create such a world, for example, is for God to be implicated in its blend of goods and evils. If God is identical with the world, as in pantheism, then God contains both goods and evils. If God is viewed as only a part of the world, then the world is metaphysically ultimate and God is not, and God is still exposed to and involved in the evils of the world by virtue of being part of the world. We have already seen how these and similar arguments go.

Only if there is no such thing as a world with any degree of distinction from God can the unambiguous goodness of a God (or some other kind of religious ultimate) seemingly be upheld. But now, since there would be nothing for God's alleged absolute goodness to relate to or be directed toward, the attribution of goodness to God becomes questionable and unclear. Advaita Vedanta Hinduism, with its claim that nothing is real but Brahman, solves this problem by denying qualities of any sort to Brahman and asserting that belief in the existence of a world independent of Brahman is *maya* or radical "misperception" of the true nature of reality. In this religious outlook, only Brahman is finally real. And nothing more can be said about Brahman than that it defies all description. The alleged reality of evil is swept away with the alleged reality of the world.

However, the presence of persistent, widespread *maya* or misperception, from the standpoint of which the reality of evil in its many forms seems overwhelmingly evident, is left without explanation. It is not clear what could be experiencing the misperception, since nothing but Brahman is said to be real, and it is not clear why there should be such a thing as *maya* in the first place. Adherents of the Advaita Vedanta version of Hinduism deal with this problem by denying any sort of relation, overlap, or commensurability—and, therefore, any sort of intelligible relation—between the realm of Brahman and that of the phenomenal world. The religious ultimate is saved from entanglement in evil by *denial of the reality of evil* and appeal to meditational states that are claimed to rise above conceptual or experiential distinctions of any kind, including distinctions between Brahman and the world and between good and evil.[2] In this book, as should by now be abundantly evident, conceptual analysis and reasoned argument have an important role to play, as do the stubborn manifestations of ordinary, day-to-day experience. In this light, the world's ambiguities and evils are all too starkly evident and real.

If we translate these ideas into the language of perspectivism, we can see that similar consequences follow. A richly perspectival and pluralistic world is going to be a world with incongruities as well as congruities, of differences as well as similarities, and of conflicts as well as of cooperation and positive interactions. Good from one perspective has the potential of being evil from another. It is good for a new species to evolve, for example, but in order for evolution to occur there must be the evil of massive extinctions. If we affirm the good from the perspective of one of the newly evolved species, *Homo sapiens*, then we must also accept the evil of vast extinctions that made its evolution possible. If we affirm the good of orderly, regular laws of nature, then we must also accept the evils experienced from the perspective of those who suffer loss and deprivation from the effects of those same laws.

Predators have a different perspective about their actions than do those upon whom they prey. And yet, without the interactions of predators and those upon whom they prey, the predators could not survive, and the prey would soon become so numerous as to have their own survival threatened. Our valuing the workings of the whole system from one perspective does not obviate the fact that from the perspective of another part of the system the evil of being constantly threatened and perhaps killed by a predator—or having the same happen to one's offspring—is the necessary concomitant of that system. The supposed good of the whole does not eclipse the evil suffered by a part of the whole. If a creator God pronounces the whole world as good from God's perspective—as is the case in the first chapter of the book of Genesis in the Hebrew Bible—it is still going to contain many aspects of potential and actual evil from the perspectives of God's creatures. One interesting sidelight to this observation is that we can interpret the biblical God to be affirming as good a world that is ambiguous, a position similar to my own affirmation of the religious rightness of nature despite its systemic natural and moral ambiguities.

If from one perspective we are grateful for the freedom of human beings and view it as essential to a meaningful life, from another we may deeply regret or fear the misuses of that freedom by some humans—misuses these humans may perceive, from their perspectives, as proper acts of freedom, in that they may regard such acts as legitimate means to their own pleasure, satisfaction, or fulfillment. This does not mean that they are right in doing so; it only means that freedom has the capacity to produce evil as well as good, mistaken as well as correct judgments, and that it makes no sense to think of having the one capacity without the other.

From the perspective of someone in a crowd where a mentally ill person is running amok with a loaded gun, it may be good that the potential mass killer is shot and killed by a policeman. In that way many lives were probably saved, perhaps including one's own life and the family members or friends by whom one is accompanied. But from the perspective of the family and friends of the potential killer, the death may be seen as a tragedy, something deeply to be regretted and mourned. And this would be so even if the family and friends came reluctantly to acknowledge the moral correctness of the policeman's action. The perspectives of intense relief, deep regret, and reluctant acknowledgment may have overlaps, but they are not completely congruent or entirely the same. Even when an evil is instrumental to an undoubted good, it remains an evil. The policeman was doing his duty, but he is right to regret having to do his duty. Taking the life of another is an evil, even though it may sometimes be necessary for the sake of what is rightly deemed to be a larger good. And judgments about whether or not something is necessary may vary, depending on the perspectives of those involved.

In a diverse, multilayered world of numerous different perspectives, it would be unreasonable to think that all of them could be satisfied in equal degree, that all of them could be equally inclusive, that all of them could be equally justified in all respects, or that there would be no honest disputes about decisions made or actions taken. The incongruities of different perspectives prohibit such outcomes, as do their differences of background, focus, and scope. Conflicts among perspectives in a richly perspectival world are inevitable. This means that what is good from one perspective may be evil from another, or that evils as viewed from one perspective will have to be countenanced for the sake of goods from other perspectives. A richly perspectival world is therefore going to be a radically ambiguous world, a necessary blend of actual and potential goods and evils. When I affirm the religious rightness of nature, I am also affirming this ambiguity and the perspectival character of reality that makes this ambiguity necessary and unavoidable.[3]

FIVE

RELIGIOUS RIGHTNESS AND MORAL VALUE

[T]he crucial religious experiences of man do not take place in a sphere in which creative energy operates without contradiction, but in a sphere in which evil and good, despair and hope, the power of destruction and the power of rebirth, dwell side by side.

—Martin Buber, *Eclipse of God*

One of the two basic kinds of evil we find pervasively present in nature is the moral evils that have been committed and continue to be committed by human beings. We have already seen that these evils can be properly regarded as evils *of nature* since humans are wholly and exclusively natural beings and are therefore integral parts of nature. The other basic kind of evil in nature is systemic natural evils. Thus, nature exhibits two kinds of ambiguity, the ambiguity of its systemic natural goods and evils and the ambiguity of its moral goods and evils. Our concern in this chapter will be with ways in which the moral ambiguity of nature relates to the unqualified religious rightness of nature I am affirming and defending throughout this book.

In order for these two appraisals of value to be consistently upheld, as we have seen, it is necessary for us to recognize two kinds of value, moral and religious value, and to seek to understand how they differ from one another and yet relate to one another. A third fundamental category of value is aesthetic value, but we will not be bringing that under explicit discussion here. What, then, is the sphere of moral value and how does it relate to the sphere of religious value? An investigation of this relationship will help us to see how a nature riddled with *moral* evils can nonetheless be conceived as *religiously* right and therefore as an appropriate focus of religious devotion. This investigation will also contribute to further disabusing ourselves of the mistaken but widespread notion that a proper object of religious concern must be free of any possible entanglement in moral ambiguity.

RELATIONS OF MORALITY AND RELIGION

One important difference between morality and religion turns on the fact that morality is solely concerned with actions that are under human control, actions that are based on discernment of the difference between moral goodness and moral evil and that are capable of choosing the good as over against the evil. A morally beneficial action is one that is intentionally performed or allowed, in accordance with moral principles and moral reasoning, and that produces as much moral goodness in a particular situation as possible. A morally reprehensible action is one that could have been avoided or prevented by a human being but that is nevertheless performed or allowed to take place, and that produces a significant amount of harm. The respective natures of moral good and moral evil are delineated in moral theories, social norms, and legal systems.

John Kekes gives us a useful characterization of moral evil in the following passage from his book *The Roots of Evil*: "[T]he evil of an action . . . consists in the combination of three components: the malevolent motivation of evildoers; the serious, excessive harm caused by their actions; and the lack of morally acceptable excuse for the actions." And he rightly reminds us that individuals may be held accountable for unintended evil consequences of their actions depending on "whether they have the motivation they ought to have, on the prevailing moral sensibility that forms part of the context of their actions, and on the foreseeable consequences of their actions" (Kekes 2005: 2, 7). They are responsible, that is to say, for the moral character and sensibility they have intentionally developed (or intentionally not developed) over time and for consequences they could have foreseen even if they did not take the trouble to foresee them.

While morality has to do with analyzing, assessing, and directing actions and consequences that are under human control, religion must take into account and find ways to cope with evil in all of its forms. One of these forms is systemic natural evils that are often beyond the power of human beings to anticipate or prevent. Religion must also help humans to find solace and meaning, strength and courage, in the face of flagrantly immoral deeds of persons or institutions that cause severe and outrageous suffering and loss—evils of which they or others are victims and which they or the others affected had no hand in committing. There may also be possibilities for good in both of these kinds of evil that religion can make us sensitive to and for which it can prepare us. Morality focuses on goods that can be brought about and evils that can be countered through human decision and effort. Religion teaches us, among other things, how to respond to evils that are not subject to our wills and that we are not able to counter or change.

Religion is also intent upon calling attention to the importance of events of grace that shower human life with goodness or possibilities for goodness but occur in ways that are beyond human prediction, manipulation, or control. These events are not outcomes of preparation or choice, but they may present opportunities for choice that were previously unexpected or nonexistent. How to be open to and how to take full advantage of the transformative possibilities of such events of grace are central religious concerns. Events of grace that lie beyond prediction or control—and sometimes far beyond what we feel worthy to experience—are a central part of what is meant by religious experience, and I submit that all genuine and profound religion is rooted in religious experience or in religious dimensions of experience. Events of grace point the way to a deepening of religious life and understanding, and they are a significant source of gratitude, hope, fortitude, and renewal. While these events transcend the ordinary, routine aspects of our lives, we need not think of them as stemming from anything supernatural. Mysterious, unexpected, and unplanned, they are seen by religion of nature as manifestations of the creative processes of nature and one way in which these ever-present, dynamic processes impact human lives. Such processes brought us into being as a species and as individuals, and as events of grace they help give us the courage to be.

These processes can become manifest in our relations to other human beings who, like ourselves, are aspects of nature, but they are not restricted to that domain. We might, for example, experience a casual meeting with someone that unexpectedly turns into a lifelong and deeply meaningful friendship. Or a teacher might have said something early in one's life, perhaps only in passing, that opened up new possibilities and set one's life on a new course. One might come across a passage in a book that points the way to new, enriching ways of thinking and acting, sometimes in respects quite different from those intended or envisioned by the book's author. Or, again, an event of grace might be an experience of being forgiven by another person or by a group of persons for a serious wrong or series of wrongs one has committed. One does not feel worthy of the forgiveness; one has not really "earned" it. It is given as a gift of grace. And one may be thereby motivated to forgive others for wrongs they have committed, and to be generally more positive and loving in one's dealings with others.

A transformative event of grace can also be the sight of a cardinal at the feeder in the back yard, a sight that we may have enjoyed in the past but that on this occasion is suddenly full of ecstatic joy and meaning. We marvel at our privilege to be living in a world that contains such exuberance, innocence, and beauty. We rejoice to think that this exquisite being, so delicately formed and colorfully arrayed, is a fellow creature with whom we are kin and with whom we share the bounty of the earth. Everything may be cast into new light and perspective by such an experience. The experience of joy and gratitude can extend to other creatures that are perhaps less brilliantly garbed or instantly admired than the cardinal (a humble house sparrow or diminutive Carolina wren, for example), but each of which contributes in its own way to the splendid vigor and variety of our planet. These experiences too can be manifestations of grace.

Even encounters with evil can sometimes be events of grace that give us new insight into the sufferings of the world against which our paltry daily frets and worries pale into insignificance. Such encounters can reorient our values and motivate us to attend to what we come to recognize as truly important. Three of Siddhartha Gautama's "Passing Sights" in his comfortable and prosperous early manhood—disease, old age, and death (the fourth sight was that of a mendicant monk)—were transformative encounters with what we have called systemic natural evils. His response to these experiences was to abandon his home and family and set out upon a wandering path of fervent study with prominent teachers of his day, begging and other austere practices, and intense religious searching that culminated in his experience of spiritual enlightenment. He thereby became the Buddha, the Enlightened One.[1]

To sum up this first point, morality is devoted to teaching us the differences between moral goodness and moral evil, and helping us to learn—through appropriate instruction, cultivation, and habituation—how consistently to choose the first as over against the second. Its focus is always on what is under our control, on what we have the capacity to do or to refrain from doing. In contrast, religion must often concern itself with goods and evils that are not under our control. These goods and evils affect our lives, sometimes decisively, and religion helps us to react to them in appropriate, constructive, and transformative ways.

It is not that religion is unconcerned with acts of human freedom and the effects of those actions. It is of course deeply concerned with such acts, and religious systems contain innumerable injunctions about how best to act in various situations, including moral situations. The point is, rather, that the scope of religious concern extends beyond instructing us about how to act morally; it includes those goods and evils that are not under our conscious control. It counsels us on how to respond to pernicious evils performed by others in such ways as to avoid total frustration, resentment, and despair, and to find positive meaning in these evils whenever possible. Finally, religion helps us to be alert and receptive to events of grace that can enrich, ennoble, and sometimes redirect our lives.

A second, closely related difference between morality and religion is that morality relates only to a part of life and the universe, while religion relates to the whole of life and the universe. Religion can help, therefore, to bring morality into the perspective of a larger whole. Religion gives us a vision of what everything adds up to, what is its ultimate significance and worth. And it gives us a vision of what our place as human beings is within the context of reality as a whole. The religious search is a search for values and modes of awareness that can provide basis, orientation, and direction for the whole course of our lives. These issues, values, and modes of awareness are closely connected with the elemental conditions of our existence as human beings: issues of birth and death, meaning and despair, good and evil, beauty and ugliness, joy and sorrow, hope and frustration, forgiveness and guilt, honor and shame.

The religious search is also a search for a sense of attunement with the secret source or sources of our being, and for the sense of responsibility and purpose that results from that sense of attunement. It seeks answers to questions such as the following: By what or whom have we come into being, and by what or whom are we most profoundly guided and sustained? What, at the most fundamental level of our lives, should we live for and aspire toward? Who are we, and what ought we to become? How can our lives be most creatively and fruitfully directed and transformed? What is to be valued above all else in the living of our lives?

Religion is also concerned with the impediments lying in the way of the creative transformation of the whole of life. Here its questions are ones such as the following: How can these impediments be recognized, dealt with, and overcome? What means of salvation or deliverance from the impediments are available to us? Where can we find a basis for hope in the face of frustration, futility, and despair? The ideals we strive for in our religious lives are not just moral values or ideals. They relate to our search for insight, inspiration, and power to heal our sense of failure and brokenness of spirit, our feelings of bewilderment and insignificance in the face of the enormity of the world, our feelings of fragmentation and lack of unifying purpose, our awareness of the chasm separating who we are from what we yearn to become.

The object of religious valuing is different, therefore, from that of moral valuing. It is a distinctive end in itself and is not subservient to some other end. What is this end? Erich Fromm joins with many other past and present thinkers in referring to the object of religious faith and devotion as the "sacred," and he emphasizes the connection of the sacred with the whole of life.

> Man's instinctual drives are necessary but trivial; man's passions that unify his energy in the search of their goal belong to the realm of the devotional or sacred. The system of the trivial is that of "making a living"; the sphere of the "sacred" is that of living beyond physical survival—it is the sphere in which man stakes his fate, often his life, the sphere in which his deepest motivations, those that make life worth living, are rooted. (Fromm, 1973: 298)

Martin Buber also insists on the bearing of religious faith and commitment upon the wholeness of life when he states, "In religious reality the person has concentrated himself into a whole, for it is only as a unified being that he is able to live religiously" (Buber 1988: 44). Moral life is encompassed in the religious vision of wholeness, sacredness, and rightness, but more than morality is involved in that vision. Moral values are not equivalent to religious values, and moral problems and concerns are not the same thing as religious problems and concerns.

It is extremely important to note, however, that morality can serve as a significant check on the outlooks and claims of religion, guarding them against the kind of fanaticism to which religious commitment sometimes tends, a fanaticism that thoughtlessly sweeps aside crucially important and relevant moral considerations in the name of unquestioning devotion to a supposed religious ultimate. History is replete with examples of the cruel and devastating effects of this kind of fanaticism. The Crusades, the Inquisition, religiously sanctioned slavery, pogroms against Jews, the attack by airplanes on the World Trade Center in New York, and individual suicide bombings in the name of Allah are examples.

The ancient story in the Hebrew Bible of Abraham's near sacrifice of his son Isaac in obedience to what he viewed as the enigmatic and yet absolutely binding command of the Lord is another example. Perhaps, as some have thought, this story marks the end, at least among the Jewish people, of the vile custom of sacrificing one's son to a god in order to placate or gain favor with the god. But the story sets a dangerous precedent of flying in the face of obvious and compelling moral values because one is convinced that God has commanded one to do so. It seems to endorse a conception of religious faith as blind, unthinking surrender to external authority that we earlier found good reason to reject. Moral principles and deeply felt moral intuitions are an important basis on which we should test the plausibility of religious demands and claims. Thus, the moral part of life can call into question a religious perspective on the whole of life or some aspect of that perspective from its own point of view, just as a religious vision of the whole of life can locate the moral part of life within a more comprehensive context and provide motivation and impetus for moral living that it might otherwise lack.

This last point suggests a third basic difference between morality and religion but also a possible connection between them. I join with many moral theorists in insisting upon the autonomy of morality. That is to say, there is no *necessary* connection between moral principles and religious beliefs. Morality has its distinctive province of interest and concern, just as religion does. It is quite possible to live a dedicated moral life without having a well-defined religious outlook. In other words, secular persons can be deeply moral persons. And moral principles and policies need not be rooted in religious principles and policies. We can note in this connection John Stuart Mill's sage response to the objection that his moral theory, Utilitarianism, is a godless doctrine because it does not derive morality from God's commands. Mill responds that Utilitarianism is *consistent* with belief in and commitment to God but does not *require* it. God can be conceived, for example, as a Utilitarian, working constantly to bring about the greatest happiness for the greatest number. This would be the sense in which we can speak of God as good. But whether or not there is a God, Mill insists that we humans should endorse, practice, and aspire toward Utilitarian ideals in our moral lives. These principles have their sanction and roots in our collective human experience (see Mill 1967: 28).

The moral philosopher R. M. Hare observes as Mill does that there can be a *contingent* connection between morality and religion even though there is no necessary one. The relation for Hare is this: moral living rests upon an unspoken faith that moral life is not futile, that we live in a universe where morality is worthwhile and can make a difference. Thus, morality operates in a larger context of assumption and meaning that it presupposes but does not itself elucidate or defend. Religion may help to provide this larger context and a more explicit basis for the hope and confidence that is so essential to moral living (see Hare 1973: 412–13). There is much in a serious and strenuous moral life that can be discouraging and even lead to a mood of futility and despair. Moral evils are rampant and deeply rooted, and we may sometimes have little sense of progress and considerable sense of failure in fighting against them. It is also possible to become deeply discouraged by evil tendencies residing in ourselves. Religious faith and the vision of the whole of life and reality it provides may help to lift us out of moods of hopelessness and futility, encouraging us to continue to have confidence that moral progress is possible and that our moral strivings continue to be worthwhile.

These strivings can be carried out in the spirit of what Buber calls an "intention of faith, intention of work out of faith," even when—contrary to his own "theonomous" way of thinking (see Buber: 98–111)—the moral principles that give them form and structure are regarded as autonomous in the sense of being self-explanatory and self-contained, and as only contingently related to any express or particular form of religious faith. One way to understand the autonomous status of morality and its contingent relation to religion is to reflect that two or more persons may often have the same, or nearly the same, moral convictions despite wide differences in their religious outlooks. Or to put the matter another way, significantly different religious outlooks can often motivate, inspire, and inform quite similar moral principles and practices. People of different faiths can thus work together for common moral goals.

In a religion of nature, there is no directive to emulate the ways of nature in one's moral life. It is not anticipated that we should reverence nature by imitating it. There is an important disconnection between the object of faith and moral policies, principles, and practices. Nature as the object of faith can provide context and support for moral living but should not be expected to supply its specific precepts. *The autonomy of morality is thus safeguarded in religion of nature.* We are not obligated or entitled, for example, to be cannibalistic because some parts of nature exhibit cannibalism. Human social life should not be dedicated to a so-called morality of the survival of the fittest, in keeping with the Social Darwinism of the late nineteenth century in the West. The poor and homeless should not simply be left to their own devices as "unfit" in a supposedly natural struggle for survival, and the strong are not entitled to prey upon the weak in the name of religion of nature. Infanticide is not sanctioned, even though it occurs in some parts of nature. And so on. Humans must develop their own ways of thinking and acting in the moral domain. What is done by instinct by some creatures is no reliable guide to what ought to be done by human beings.

In the perspective of religion of nature, human beings are a species with consciousness, intelligence, and freedom. They are expected to learn from their historical experience and from their critical, constructive reasoning and thought how to live together in harmony and how to structure their social lives in ways that conduce to justice and fairness for all. There might be potential moral lessons of the nonhuman parts of nature to be taken to heart, for example, the model of many diverse creatures living together and supporting one another in complexly entwined ecosystems as a model of how to live in a pluralistic society. (We would have to eliminate the routine predatory practices from the model that are an essential part of ecological dependencies in nature.) But the basic point is that slavish imitation of the nonhuman parts of nature in our moral lives is out of the question.

The philosopher Bernard Rollin notes that "it stands to reason that certain moral principles would evolve in all societies as a minimum requirement for living together. Any society with property would need prohibitions against stealing; communication necessitates prohibitions against lying; murder could certainly not be freely condoned; and so on." He makes a convincing case for the thesis that moral values were arrived at by human beings on the basis of their reason and experience as they endeavored over time to find ways to live safely and productively together, and that some moral values are probably common to all cultures simply because they are essential to a stable social existence. Rollin wryly observes that even "a band of robbers . . . must presuppose some rules of conduct governing their conduct toward one another, or they could accomplish nothing" (Rollin 2006: 49, 45, ch. 3 *passim*). So there is no more need in religion of nature to think of ethics as having to be derived from the nonhuman aspects of nature than there is to believe that it must descend from on high in the form of mandates from a transcendent deity or deities. I am in entire agreement with Rollin's contention that the essential and most basic features of social ethics are rooted in what becomes apparent to human reason as it takes into account the need for consistency, coherence, and comprehensiveness in moral principles and moral practice, and as it wrestles with the stern lessons of human historical experience. The idea of an autonomous human ethics, that is, one that is not tied necessarily to the specifics of any particular religious outlook, is therefore perfectly consistent with religion of nature.

However, the moral sensitivity and practice of reflective, historically seasoned humans should be extended beyond the human sphere to include the other creatures of nature. For the latter, like ourselves, are entitled to conscientious moral consideration and treatment. As we saw earlier, human social ethics should be considered a subset of ecological ethics, an ethics that encompasses all living creatures and exhibits profound respect for every feature of their natural environments. In the perspective of religion of nature, therefore, moral principles and practices are not to be *derived* from nonhuman nature, but they are most certainly to be *applied* to it. Humans are part of a much larger community of all the creatures of earth, and it is essential that they work to keep their part of nature in balance and harmony with the other parts of this natural community.

We can and should work within the whole of nature to bring about moral good and to avoid needless suffering and harm. But we must also be aware that our actions as humans are a relatively small part of an enormous system, and we must be on guard lest we overestimate the importance of our human lives and actions within that system. The religious life can be a striving to change what can be changed for the moral good. But it must also be composure and acceptance in the face of things that cannot be changed and should not changed for the sake of the system of nature as a whole. Gaining such composure and acceptance is a central religious goal and a vital part of understanding the meaning of the religious rightness of nature.

Nature's rightness does not merely involve me, those nearest to me, or even all of my fellow human creatures, even though it certainly does in part. Keen and humble awareness of this fact is essential for genuine reverence and respect for nature as a whole. We should work to cultivate such self-effacing but appreciative awareness within ourselves. We can do so by religiously inspired deeds of kindness and mercy toward all creatures; by meditation, prayer, ritual, and other forms of public and private religious practice; by reflecting frequently upon the vastness of the universe in space and time; and by careful observation and study of the intricacies and interconnections of the myriad life forms on this planet. We can also be open to possible further deepening of this awareness by events of grace that may steal in upon our consciousness and transform our outlooks and lives in unexpected ways—especially if we have sought to prepare ourselves earlier for effective response to such events when they occur. Nature in its panoplied splendor can be marveled at and celebrated. But confrontation with its staggering might can also evoke eerie feelings of trepidation and awe, together with an overpowering sense of our own puniness and vulnerability in the face of that might. A religion of nature helps to put the moral life in the perspective of a larger whole, a perspective that accepts the inevitability of systemic evils and the possibility of moral evils in order that systemic goods can occur and in order that the freedom to work for moral goodness can be present.

MORAL GOODNESS, RELIGIOUS RIGHTNESS, AND THE AMBIGUITY OF NATURE

I wanted to examine in some detail the different domains of morality and religion, and to say something about the interrelations of these two domains, in order further to clarify in this manner the basic distinction I am drawing in this book between the concept of religious rightness, on the one hand, and the concept of moral goodness, on the other. Let me try now to summarize what I mean by religious rightness. Some of what I say here I have said before, but I want to draw it all together in one place so as to provide as clear a statement as I can of what religious rightness amounts to when applied to nature. Having done that, and having in the previous section talked more generally about some of the relations of morality and religion, I can conclude this chapter by indicating specifically how religion and morality relate to the ambiguities of nature and to the case I am developing for the aptness of nature as the object of religious faith.

For religion of nature, contemplation and practice of the rightness of nature mean affirming both the metaphysical and the religious ultimacy of nature. It is inquiring deeply into our appropriate place within the whole of nature and living gratefully and responsibly with that sense of appropriateness. It is giving of ourselves for the well-being of the earth and all its constituents and systems. It is finding inspiration in the marvels of nature. It is glorying in the starry heavens, the sparkling seas, the rushing rivers, the stalwart mountains, the far-flung plains, and all the marvelous life forms of earth, large and small. It is stupefying wonder in the presence of the mysteries of nature. It is delight in the beauties of nature and reverent meditation on nature's complexity, majesty, and splendor. It is gratitude for the providingness of the earth and feeling at home here, with no need to pine for something beyond the earth or beyond nature as a whole. It is an abiding sense of companionship and kinship with all the creatures in our natural home, human and nonhuman alike.

Envisioning and practicing the rightness of nature in a religion of nature is also learning courage and patience in the presence of what is not within our power to change. It is giving thanks for the consciousness, intelligence, and freedom that nature has bestowed upon us as a species and learning to use these gifts effectively and responsibly. It is working to alleviate needless suffering and pain and finding ways to contribute to—but also to avoid undue interference with—the flourishing of all of earth's creatures. It is being open and receptive to events of grace, to the lessons to be learned from them and the transformative possibilities inherent within them. It is joy in family and friends. It is experiencing support, motivation, and strength in religious community and working in religious community for the betterment of the world. Moral obligations of various kinds are critically important in this religious vision of rightness, but more than morality is involved in it. Acceptance of moral ambiguities in nature as the focus of religious faith is an essential part of this vision, as are understanding and accepting the inevitability of systemic natural evils.

Understood in these ways, the ambiguities of nature present no barrier to its being regarded as the focus of religious faith. We should not expect nonhuman nature to exemplify moral principles or to provide, in and of itself, a path for moral living. Nor should we expect it to exhibit only systemic natural goods. Nature must permit moral evils in order to bestow its gift of human freedom. It requires systemic natural evils as well as systemic natural goods in order to function as it does, and in order that humans can have meaningful exercise of their freedom. Religious rightness does not demand unambiguous moral rightness in its object of religious commitment, nor does it imply a total absence of natural calamities or harms in such an object.

The ambiguities of nature qualify it as a focus of religious faith because without these ambiguities nature would have to be like the world we tried to imagine in a previous chapter. It would be flat, fixed, uninteresting, and unchallenging. There would be no such thing as genuine creativity or novelty in such a world. The imagined world would make human life meaningless because all possible goods would already have been achieved and there would nothing for humans to strive for or to accomplish. In addition, there would be no such thing as freedom and its risks; humans would be automata, living out preprogrammed lives. It is not even clear that such a world can be imagined. But it is clear that even if we could imagine it, we would not want to live in it. I presented strong reasons for this conclusion earlier.

The ambiguities of nature are not only consistent with its being viewed as religiously right. They are *necessary* if it is to be a fit object of religious reverence and devotion. We should rejoice in these ambiguities even as we struggle with them and seek to avoid or prevent as far as possible their evil effects. The religious path of religion of nature is not a simple or easy path, but it is an eminently suitable path for us human creatures of nature. This path is fraught with mystery, uncertainty, and danger. There is much about nature and our lives as natural beings we can never hope fully to understand. The spiritual path of religion of nature combines sober realism about the destructive systemic and deplorable moral evils of the world with glad acknowledgment of the wide-ranging systemic and moral goods it also contains and the transformative goods it makes possible. This path demands commitment of our entire selves throughout our lives and the never-ending search for a comprehensive vision of the world and our place within it. Religious rigor combines with moral rigor in a religion of nature. When they are properly understood, neither conflicts in general with the other, even though each belongs to a distinctive domain of thought, aspiration, and experience. The full resources of both are needed in the battle against moral evils, in coping with systemic natural evils, and in attuning ourselves with the motivations and powers of nature-centered religious rightness.

SIX

COPING WITH AMBIGUITY

> [E]very religious perspective, with its mythology, rituals, symbols, and rhetoric is implicitly a theodicy in the broad sense of the term. It not only provides means by which to accommodate or transform meaningless suffering; it provides a framework in which to *understand* it, to *explain* its origins, to *offer* resolutions, and to *recommend* responses.
>
> —Tyron L. Inbody, *The Transforming God*

I deeply concur with the spirit of Tyron Inbody's observation. It expresses an important truth and perhaps *the* most important truth that we need always to keep in mind when thinking or talking about religion. "Theodicy," however, is too provincial a term to use in this connection because of its explicit reference to God (Grk: *theos*). Not all religious perspectives focus on God, and we should be careful to avoid terminology that suggests otherwise, however familiar or well intended the terminology may be. We need a broader, more inclusive concept because every viable system of religious beliefs and practices, whether theistic or not, must have *at its heart* ways of interpreting and responding to the tragic dimensions of life and of providing hope, strength, and meaning to fortify us for encounters with evil. The broader analogue to a God-centered theodicy, then, is examination of the fundamental issue of how any given religious system relates to the menace of evil and the extent to which it provides illuminating, trustworthy, usable resources for understanding and coping with this menace in all of its forms.

At its deepest level, horrible sufferings of body or spirit are dark and inexplicable, and it would be naïve to suggest otherwise. Religious explanations can go some way in accounting for them, but not all the way. This is as true of religion of nature, in the final analysis, as it is of any other religious outlook. Conceptual explanations of systemic natural and moral evils such as those I have provided earlier can help us to cope with evil but they will always be insufficient by themselves. Coping with the world's ambiguities calls for responses that reach beyond theoretical levels of comprehension to existential, emotional, and spiritual depths of the soul. These depths are finally as mysterious in their workings and powers as are the grave evils of rampant destructiveness, intense suffering, monstrous cruelty, callous exploitation, and the like that require their response.

Religious systems help us to plumb these depths by seeking to provide as much conceptual explanation as they can, but also by evoking with symbol, rite, meditation, myth, parable, koan, and story the courageous life-affirming powers of the human spirit—powers nature has implanted, by all indications, in each and every living being. The philosopher Hannah Arendt wisely observes, "Storytelling reveals meaning, without committing the error of defining it."[1] To be fully effective, religious systems and traditions must draw deeply upon the revelatory powers of symbol and story. My discussions in this book will continue to be mostly on the level of theory and conceptual explanation, but I hope that they will shed light upon the positive, sustaining, saving side of nature's ambiguities and provide a framework that points beyond itself to sources of assurance and affirmation that lie within us and within the world, but that elude the clear grasp of concept and theory.

There are those who would view the conceptual framework of religion of nature as unhelpful in the extreme, who would castigate it for its lack of reference to God or the realm of the supernatural, and who would be strongly tempted to brand it as a thinly disguised nihilism. I want to examine in this chapter the sort of case these thinkers might make for this conclusion, to explain why the case does not hold, and to indicate how religion of nature can enable us to cope effectively with nature's ambiguities and the menace of evil. Let us look first, then, at arguments for the claim that religion of nature is a thinly disguised nihilism, a nihilism that gives us no genuine help for living in the face of nature's ambiguities. Then we shall consider the case that can be made for religion of nature in response to these arguments and in defense of its adequacy as a way of dealing with the threats of evil in the world. If religion of nature cannot meet the fundamental test of its competency to deal with these threats—stubborn, pervasive, and ominous as they undoubtedly are—then it does not deserve serious consideration as a possible focus of religious faith. The present chapter is a litmus test of that competency and as such constitutes what I consider to be the most crucial chapter of this book.

NIHILISTIC DESPAIR

Nihilism can be succinctly defined as despair of the finite. In many of its forms, it is at bottom the view that if there is nothing infinite upon which the finite depends or points beyond itself to affirm, then the finite is meaningless and absurd.[2] Human life is thought to be meaningless, for example, if it does not extend infinitely into the future. A life that culminates in a finality of death is regarded as an absurd life. There must be an infinite being, that is, one that exists necessarily and possesses all imaginable perfections of power, consciousness, wisdom, purpose, and goodness, and that is the source and sustainer of the finite world. This being must give ultimate purpose and meaning to the world and to human life; otherwise, neither can have purpose or meaning. This being must reside in a separate world from the finite natural world; that is, it must reside in a *supernatural* world whose infinite, unambiguous, impregnable perfection contrasts radically with the finitude and imperfection of the natural world. This being must communicate with us from its supernatural realm in the form of definitive revelations and other kinds of disclosure, and we must be able to enter into personal relations with it through prayer and meditation. It must respond to our prayers and grant healing power and direction for our lives.

This being must be the source and dispenser of moral absolutes; otherwise, there can be no binding moral principles. This infinite being must also give absolute assurance of the supremacy of goodness over evil; otherwise, there can be no hope that living in accordance with moral ideals can make a fundamental difference in human life or the world. And it must confer upon human beings a status and dignity—a special importance in the whole scheme of things—that is not possessed by any other creature. Otherwise, human beings are reduced to the status of beasts. Finally, this infinite being must be infinitely knowledgeable and wise. It must not be restricted in any way from total understanding of everything in the universe, past, present, or future. Truth among humans is to be seen as correspondence to, approximation to, or reflection of aspects of the absolute, all-encompassing epistemic vision of the infinite being.

Nihilists find themselves able to affirm *none* of these things even though they assume them to be *essential*. They have come to the sad conclusion that finitude is the whole story of the universe and of human life within the universe. Since this is true, they then draw the further conclusion that the universe is without point, purpose, or meaning, and that human life is absurd. In this event, there can be no unconditional truths or absolute moral standards. There is no basis for hope. There is no protection against the ravages of evil. There is no refuge from ambiguity. There is no providential care over the world to give meaning to suffering. There is no infinite being with conscious, purposive care over the world with whom humans can enter into personal relations, to whom they can direct their prayers of praise, gratitude, and petition, and from whom they can draw guidance and support. There is no afterlife of everlasting bliss to compensate the innocent for their sufferings, to reward the just for their persistence in goodness, or to give assurance of reunion with loved ones beyond the grave. Nihilism's despair of the finite is more properly characterized as despair of *the absence of the infinite*—as the unquestioned supposition or belief that, without rootage in the infinite and without ultimate reference or recourse to it, nothing finite can have any meaning. And since, for the nihilist, the infinite can nowhere be found, or at least belief in it and commitment to it are always open to serious question, criticism, or doubt, everything is deemed to be absurd.

RELIGION OF NATURE'S RESPONSE

If we accept this reasoning, which I do not, then religion of nature would seem to be a form of nihilism. For it does indeed deny the sorts of infinitude referred to in the nihilist's analysis. The only kind of infinity assumed in religion of nature is an infinity of endless and inexhaustible change, the everlasting workings of nature naturing. The workings of cosmic creation are also, as we have seen, workings of destruction. They are therefore ambiguous in their very nature. Furthermore, they lack consciousness, purposiveness, or providential care. They give rise to all things finite but also, in the fullness of time, lead inevitably to their destruction. Time itself is a blend of creation and destruction, because it must leave the past behind in order to make room for the newness and difference of the present and future. Since it sets forth a vision of life and the universe in which there is no cosmic purpose, no infinite being, no escape from ambiguity, no creation without destruction, no everlasting human life, no refuge from the ceaseless gnawings of time, no moral or epistemological absolutes, no unqualified guarantees of the ultimate meaningfulness of suffering or of the final triumph of good over evil, is religion of nature in its very nature a recipe for despair?

It is so only if we accept the crucial assumption that *if* there is nothing infinite (save the relentless workings of change, as represented most comprehensively in nature naturing), *then* the finite can have no meaning. But is this hypothetical statement really true? Does its antecedent entail its consequent? Religion of nature flatly denies that it does, thus taking fundamental issue with the heart of the nihilist's reasoning. Far from despairing of the finite, religion of nature *affirms* the finitude of all things possible or real and asserts—though with full acknowledgment of the tragic aspects of reality—the adequacy of the finite as the context for human life, for the lives of other beings, and for whatever takes place in the world. It is not, then, in either affirmation or implication, a form of nihilism.

Religion of nature's message of assurance and hope is laced with sober awareness of the sufferings, sorrows, disappointments, and terrors of life in the world, for these things are manifestations of the finite world's ambiguities. But its message is also deeply informed by all that is good in the world, by all that is fascinating, beautiful, hopeful, joyful, sustaining, rejuvenating, saving, and life-affirming. This is the other side of the world's ambiguities. Seeing things in this way, we can now redefine nihilism as despair of the finite not only because of absence of the infinite, but also as the result of focusing on *only one side*—the evil, precarious, frustrating, frightening side—of the ambiguities of the world. Another mistake of the nihilist view is thinking that all good is completely separable from evil, that there can be such a thing as wholesale unambiguous goodness or absolute safety. Religion of nature calls into question this one-sided focus and unanalyzed assumption.

If we grant, then, that religion of nature is not a form of nihilism from its own perspective because it takes issue with crucial assumptions and directions of thought upon which the kind of nihilism we have described rests, how does religion of nature propose that we cope with evil? Can it find adequate resources within the ambiguities of human life and the world to take fully into account, find consoling and motivating meaning in, and deal effectively with the systemic natural and moral evils that threaten humans and other parts of nature at every turn? Is the finite enough, or must there be infinites and absolutes upon which it rests and upon which finite beings such as ourselves must rely in order to find sufficient succor and strength? Can religion of nature make a *successful case* for its contention that, without appeals to unambiguous infinites and absolutes, the finite world can provide ample purpose and meaning, and finite human life can be genuinely worthwhile?

Questions such as these are the concerns of the next two sections. The preceding chapters of this book presented or adumbrated ways of responding to questions of this kind, but I want now to recall and amplify these responses and bring them to bear on the central issue of how we can find meaning in our lives and discover ways to cope conceptually, practically, and spiritually with the ambiguities of nature. This means, above all else, learning how to deal hopefully, constructively, and effectively with the manifestations of evil in nonhuman nature, with the reckless perversities that lie within the human breast, and with the daunting trials and injuries these perversities inflict upon the lives of humans and nonhumans alike.

FINITE LIFE AND EXISTENTIAL MEANING

In this section I present some responses of religion of nature to the nihilist's claim that human life can have no meaning if only the finite exists and there is nothing infinite upon which life rests and to which it points. In the section to follow, I respond to the contention that resources of finite life by themselves are patently inadequate to enable us to deal with the systemic natural and moral evils of the world. One reason offered in defense of the first claim is that if the universe has no overarching *purpose* conferred upon it from without by some kind of world-transcending conscious creator, or from within by some type of immanent purposive being, then human life within such a universe can have no meaning. Meaningful human purposes, in other words, require that we live in a world whose existence exhibits, derives from, and is informed by the intention and design of an ultimate purposive being. Our human purposes can be validated only in the context of a discoverable purpose for the cosmos as a whole.

This alleged connection between an ultimate cosmic purpose and finite human purposes is not at all clear, and it seems by no means to be necessary. Why must human purposes be validated by cosmic purpose in order to be satisfying, meaningful, or real? Why do we need the context of an overarching purpose of the universe as a whole in order to find purposes for the living of our lives? The universe has brought us into being as purposive agents, but it need not itself be a purposive agent in order to do so. In fact, the current evolutionary model of this universe's origin and of the origin of humans and other life forms is a model in which consciousness and purposiveness are emergent rather than primordial phenomena.[3]

With a high order of biological complexity, purposive activity becomes possible in us and other natural beings, but it did not become possible until that high order of complexity was developed through eons of evolutionary changes and adaptations. Once developed, though, purposive activity follows as a matter of course. Beings capable of this activity have such purposes as seeking their survival and protecting the appropriate ways of life for themselves and their progeny. They have the purposes of their many daily pursuits and endeavors. In the case of us humans, we have potentially rich purposes made possible by such things as our high level of conscious awareness, our development of complex languages and cultures, and our ability to imagine, construct, and innovate in domains such as science, technology, the humanities, and the arts. There is also the ever-present moral challenge and purpose of striving to learn how to live with one another and with other creatures of nature in mutual concord and harmony. Even without an infinite, these purposes remain, and they continue to be valid and important. They are integral to our lives as the kind of highly developed, complex organism we are.

There is more than a trace of anthropocentrism in the idea that the universe must be the outcome of conscious purpose. We tend to assume that it must be based on or originate within a mind such as ours, with explicitly intended rational purposes and designs. We do not stop to consider that these capacities in us may be one of many different waves of evolutionary development that have rippled out from the earliest life forms in all directions and that are not themselves initially guided by consciousness or purpose. We further assume that such conscious purposes and designs must be traits of an infinite being basically similar to us, but with human-like capacities elevated or expanded to an infinite degree. We dismiss out of hand the possibility that the finite is itself the cause and principle behind everything, in which case it makes more sense to say that the finite is itself ultimate—that is, there is nothing beyond or beneath it—than to insist that the finite must be rooted in an infinite ultimate. If so, then we can conclude that the universe becomes conscious of itself in its conscious creatures here on earth and, in all probability, elsewhere in the cosmos as well. That is to say, over vast stretches of time it comes to be endowed with consciousness and purpose in finite beings with these evolved capacities, and it is not necessary for us to think that the universe as a whole must stem from or be guided by a primordial cosmic consciousness.

Even when we speak of nature naturing, we are not talking about something that exists independently of finite processes, entities, and principles that come into being and pass away, but simply about manifestations of the dynamic operations and interrelations of these processes, entities, and principles. To talk of nature naturing is to give a name to endless processes of creation and destruction that mark the present universe and have been and will continue to be operative in universes of the past and future, if we think there is reason to believe, as I do, that there have been and will be such. It is to make reference to an infinite *temporal span* of these processes but not to suggest any other kinds of infinitude to be associated with them. Thus, the temporal infinitude of nature naturing, that is, the everlasting processive character of the universe (or universes), is just that and nothing more. It does not imply or require other kinds of infinitude such as all-encompassing knowledge, perfect goodness, absolute power, or a comprehensive purpose conferred upon the world by an infinite being.

But then, it might be objected, there is no *sufficient reason* for the existence of the universe or for its character as the realization of one set of possibilities rather than another set. Hence, the very being of the universe is rendered unintelligible and absurd, and life in such a universe cannot help but be finally absurd. There are two responses I want to make to this objection. The first is my contention as a proponent of religion of nature that the universe is its own reason, its own explanation. The universe is the context within which all explanations take place, the starting point or given from which all explanations flow. Explanations cannot regress forever and still count as explanations. They must start some place. For religion of nature, the finite universe is their appropriate starting place. We can account to a considerable extent for the present character of the universe by drawing upon what we can extrapolate or deduce about its past or previous characters. But there is no compelling need for us to arrive at a definitive explanation for the fact of there being some sort of universe in the first place.

There seems to be a tacit assumption implicit in the demand for an explanation or reason for the existence of the universe itself. The assumption, often unrecognized and unanalyzed, is that nothingness is a more natural state of things than somethingness. Therefore, there is a heavy burden upon us to explain why there is something rather than nothing. But sheer nothingness is unintelligible. Why should we assume that it is a more natural state than somethingness? Even to speak of it as a "state" is to attribute some kind of existence to it and thus to contradict the claim of its being nothing. And what could the contradictory phrase "being nothing" mean?

Nothingness is a privative conception, the negation of something positive or existing that might have been present but that is not in some particular case. For this absence to make sense, there must be a broader background of existing things within which the absence of some particular thing or type of thing can be conceived. Without existence of some kind within which the relative privation of some aspect of that existence takes place or can be imagined, the concept of nothingness loses its meaning.

So, far from nothingness being the natural state of things, the alternative to which (somethingness) requires explanation, the real situation is exactly the opposite. Negation is meaningless unless there is already something to be negated. Hence, total negation or sheer nothingness is unintelligible. All negation is partial and derivative, while the existence of a universe or of some kind of antecedent reality is primordial. If we consider the antecedent reality to be an infinite being such as God, then either for God's existence the question, "Why this, rather than nothing?" must still be raised, involving us again in the problem of the unintelligibility of sheer nothingness, or we must simply accept the existence of God as primordial, as the given on the basis of which all else is to be finally explained. This is what religion of nature does with the existence of the universe. Explanations can culminate with the givenness of a universe of some sort and need go no farther.

My second response to the objection now under consideration is that there is no reason to think that everything in the universe must be intelligible through and through. The present face of the universe is the outcome of two factors: causal laws and novel contingencies. These novel contingencies or workings of chance are not intelligible through and through for the simple reason that the intelligibility of cosmic processes requires their explanation in terms of regular, predictable causal laws, and factors of chance are not amenable to explanation in terms of causal laws. And yet, without the interrelations of chance and law, the universe as we know it today could not have evolved. Moreover, if there was no such thing as chance, there would no openness of the future within which human freedom could operate and make a difference.

Chance occurrences take place within the context of causal laws, but they are not made wholly explicable by those laws. Hence, not everything about the universe is susceptible, even in principle, to causal explanation. This means that not everything is susceptible to *complete* explanation. There is no such thing as the "principle of sufficient reason" envisioned by the Enlightenment philosopher Gottfried Leibniz[4] that can account for the past, present, or future character of the universe as a whole. A dynamic universe is made possible by the blend of the regularity of efficient causes and the unpredictability of chance. Continuity and novelty work together, meaning that some aspects of the workings of the universe are always going to be contingent and surprising, and opaque to causal explanation both in fact and in principle.[5] Thus, the universe is not made completely absurd by the lack of a principle of sufficient reason to explain its existence and character, nor is human life thereby rendered absurd. On the contrary, if the principle of sufficient reason did apply to the universe as a whole, human freedom would be nonexistent and human life would be stripped of purpose and significance.

Shifting now to another aspect of the nihilist's case, the nihilist's allegation that human life is absurd if it ends in death and does not enter finally into a supernatural realm beyond the grave that brings endless contentment, fulfillment, and peace, unmixed with any possibility of suffering, frustration, mistake, or evil, is vulnerable to at least three critical responses. The first is that this supernatural realm sounds like the perfect world we tried earlier to imagine and found to be not only extremely difficult to conceive but highly undesirable for beings like us. This is so perhaps most clearly in that we could have no genuine freedom in such an afterlife, and that its alleged absolute, completely realized perfection would require nothing of us. In the absence of any challenge or effort on our part, or any need for our particular choices and actions, it is hard to see how we could regard our lives as meaningful or worthwhile.

Another response to this allegation of the nihilist is that it uncritically assumes that, in order for something to be worthwhile, it must endure forever. The logic of this claim is not at all clear. The universe is a place of ceaseless change, and the procession of our experiences undergoes change from moment to moment and day to day. We change in fundamental ways as we go from infancy to old age. Most of what has occurred to us in the past is no longer retained in our conscious memories. We did not exist infinitely into the past, and there is no clear reason why it is necessary for us to live infinitely into the future. There are many experiences that we can cherish and enjoy, and in which we can find deep challenge and fulfillment, even though we know full well that they will not last forever. In fact, our knowledge that they will not last forever can impart to them a special kind of urgency, vividness, value, and importance. Our lives need not last forever in order to be meaningful.

But what about compensating the innocent who suffer and rewarding the just? Is not some sort of afterlife required to balance the accounts and to provide assurance of the ultimate triumph of goodness over evil? My third response is a reply to these questions. For one thing, such a view assumes the *conceivability* and *desirability* of an afterlife of perfect, unambiguous bliss. And we have called those two assumptions into question. Moreover, it is not at all clear how a future lifetime of bliss could "compensate" the innocent for the sufferings of this life, especially when those sufferings are exceptionally grievous and extensive. In saying this, I do not mean to detract from the profound feelings of lament we rightly feel and should feel for the sufferings of the innocent. It is precisely such feelings that entitle us to question the idea of an ultimately satisfactory compensation for those sufferings in an afterlife. As for rewarding the just, perhaps justice is best understood as its own reward. To do the good simply because it is good is meaningful in and of itself. Finally, this view tends to take the focus off of dealing with evils here and now by seeming to lessen our duty to defend the innocent *in the present* from unmerited suffering, to deter and punish evildoers, and to fight against evil institutions. It can make evils seem less glaring and disturbing, and less in need of immediate, firm, resolute response, when we confront them with an underlying assurance that they will eventually be *inevitably* righted in an afterlife.

For religion of nature, there is no absolute guarantee of the triumph of good over evil in particular situations, and there certainly can be no possibility of the elimination of evil altogether, given the ambiguous relations of good and evil that we have examined elsewhere. But such acknowledgments do not entail the conclusion that life is absurd. To say that there is no guarantee is to say that the future is not fixed and therefore that no outcome is inevitable. Instead, the future is open to us and in significant need of our efforts and accomplishments, including our struggles against evil here and now. This realization would seem to *add* meaning to our lives rather than subtracting meaning from them.

We can turn next to the nihilist's insistence that we must be special beings, with a special status and dignity, and a special importance in the scheme of things. Otherwise, or so it is argued, we are reduced to the status of beasts. Here we witness again the camel's nose of an arrogant anthropocentrism poking into the tent of our status as natural beings. In response, we can note that all species are special. Their being special is another way of speaking of the distinctiveness of each one of them as species. Our difference as humans from other creatures of the earth is relative, not absolute, a difference of degree, not of kind.[6] We are animals and, like other animals, we depend crucially upon such things as the warmth and energy of the sun; the photosynthesis of plants and their place within the food chain; the water in the clouds, rivers, and seas; the fertility of the soil; the microbes and minerals in the ground and in our bodies; the intricate relations of species, including our own, with one another and with their natural environments; and the laws of nature. To acknowledge these facts is not to demean us or to denigrate our status in the scheme of things. It is to celebrate our participation in the community of creatures, our oneness with the earth, and the privilege of our being at home here. We do not have to belong in our essential nature to some supernatural realm, nor do we have to be created in the image and likeness of a supernatural being in order to live a satisfactory and fulfilling life.

This last statement brings us to another one of the nihilist's assumptions with which we can take issue. That assumption is that our lives are

meaningless if they cannot be guided and protected by the providential care
of an infinite being, and if we cannot enter into personal relations with
that being through prayers of praise, thankfulness, confession, and petition.
Our lives are thought to be too precarious for us to make it through on
our own or by the help we can extend to one another. We need the help
and strength of a higher power. The nihilist concludes that there is no such
power and therefore also concludes that the course of our lives is nothing
more than the plaything of impersonal, capricious, taunting fortune. With
no personal, loving, infinitely wise spirit to help us in times of trouble and
need, and to respond to our desperate prayers for direction and help, our
lives are deemed to be pointless, and we are judged by the nihilist to be
doomed to despair.

I respect these contentions. They reflect the faith of millions of people
living on the face of this earth. People do find strength and help through
their faith in a God to whom they can turn in prayer and with whom they
feel themselves to be in communion. But I do not personally find compelling reasons to believe in or to put my faith in such a God, and I do not
accept the argument that the absence of such a God means that we must
abandon hope and succumb to despair. For one thing, each of us is not
hopelessly alone and devoid of help. We have each other, and we have
this whole wonderful world in which to live our lives. We can give thanks
for the gifts of this world, we can confess our sins and aspire with the help
of others to live better lives and become better persons, and we can sing
hymns of praise for the beauty of the earth. We can rejoice in the events
of grace that bless our lives and seek ways to respond to these events so as
to take maximum advantage of the opportunities they confer upon us. We
can find meaning in helping others and in working to enhance and preserve
our natural environment and the lives of all of the creatures within it. We
can work to eradicate those evils that can be eradicated and seek ways to
accept with humility, courage, and composure those that cannot. I will speak
further about this last matter in the next section.

What about petitionary prayer? Do not many of us, at least in many
parts of the world, find ourselves turning to some kind of deity in our times
of desperate anxiety, feelings of helplessness, and deepest longing? And do
we not instinctively feel the need for some kind of infinite personal power
to whom we can direct our prayers for guidance, solace, and strength? The
idea of our need for such a deity is deeply engrained in the cultures of
much of the world, so it is not surprising that this need in persons reared
in those cultures might seem to be instinctive or even to provide some sort
of validation for the reality of the object of that need. But one's felt need
does not entail the existence of the thing for which one might yearn. A
person lost in the desert has a desperate need for water, but that does not
mean that the water is thereby made available. Wishing that something is
true does not make it true. Therefore, the desire for a deity to whom we

can pray in times of need—no matter how deeply rooted that desire might be—does not mean that such a deity must really exist.

The very notion of petitionary prayer is not without its problems, as has often been observed. A deity who depends on petitionary prayer to do good, who must in that way be *persuaded* to do good, is not a worshipful deity. Is such a deity a kind of aloof despot who must be placated, cajoled, begged to do good? Must we lavish praise upon the deity before it can decide finally, and perhaps reluctantly, to address our legitimate needs or the other kinds of legitimate need we implore it to notice? Without our prayers, does the deity *forget* to do the good things it ought to do?

It is a well-known fact, moreover, that petitionary prayers do not always work as they are intended to do, no matter how pious or persistent the one doing the praying may be, or how appropriate the prayers may seem to be. No doubt many prayers were raised during the flu pandemic of 1918–19 or the tsunami of 2004, but large numbers of those who prayed or were prayed for still died. The same was true for the countless prayers of Jews and others separated from their families and being killed or wasting away in the death camps of the Third Reich. And many mothers who have prayed earnestly for the safety of their military sons (or daughters) engaged in war have received telegrams announcing the sad news of their children's deaths in battle. So perhaps the only kind of petitionary prayer that really makes sense, even if we assume the existence of an infinite being who presides over the world, is the prayer "Thy will be done." If so, petitionary prayer becomes the search for attunement with and acceptance of the will of the deity, whatever that will might turn out to be. This is in all probability good for the person or persons doing the praying, but it is not likely to alter or redirect the will of a truly loving, benevolent, all-knowing deity.

But at least, it might be objected, there is *meaning* in suffering, sorrow, disappointment, and evil in a universe presided over by an infinite deity. At least that being knows what it is doing and does everything for the best. But note that this confidence does not detract from the enigmatic character of the sufferings and evils themselves, nor has it done anything to prevent them. There may be meanings in the sufferings, but we have no way of knowing what they are. So the situation of one who has faith in God is not all that different from one who does not. From our finite human perspective, the frustrations and mysteries of suffering and evil still remain.

If we probe a bit deeper, we can also see that the vast extent of the evils of the world and the huge numbers of persons and other creatures who suffer grievous harm from these evils can lead us to wonder if the world is really presided over by a loving, benevolent, all-knowing deity and, if so, why it allows so much terrible evil to exist. There is a sense in which the universe is made *more* in danger of becoming meaningless and absurd, upon reflection, if such a deity is said to exist than if it does not. This is the predicament of Job and of all persons of traditional theistic faith who suffer from deeply regretful and seemingly needless evils.

Why does an assumedly just God who is believed to be in complete charge of the universe and all that happens within it *inflict* grave evils upon Job in a seemingly arbitrary manner, or at least stand aside and *permit* horrendous sufferings of body and soul to torment him? To this question, no finally satisfying answer is given in the Book of Job or elsewhere in the Hebrew Bible. At the end of the Book of Job, its central character finally resigns himself to trusting without question in mysterious ways of God that he is counseled by God himself must remain forever hidden and unintelligible to Job and other mere mortals.[7] In contrast, a religion of nature is not required to puzzle about how claims to the absolute goodness and omnipotence of God can be reconciled with the pervasive evils of the world. It still has to struggle with these evils in its own manner, but its position in this regard is no more absurd and perhaps in some important respects less absurd than that of those who place their uncomprehending faith in an infinite being.

The next set of arguments and claims of the nihilist to which I want to respond includes the claim that humans are in need of definitive revelations of what is ultimately true and what is false about the world from an infinite being residing in a supernatural realm, especially when it comes to matters of faith and morals. This being is said to be infinitely wise, and therefore a completely trustworthy source of knowledge, and the dispenser of absolute moral standards that reflect its infinite goodness. According to the nihilist, only such a being who is not restricted in any way from a total understanding of the universe in all its aspects can be a reliable source of knowledge and understanding. The nihilist further alleges that our own claims to knowledge and understanding can qualify as such only to the extent that they correspond to or at least closely approximate the all-comprehending vision of the world possessed by such a being. In the absence of such a being, or so the nihilist claims, we can have no confidence in any of our convictions about knowledge or value. If there are no unconditional truths or absolute moral standards, communicated to us and sanctioned from the vantage point of an infinite being's all-seeing eye, then claims to truth and value are without foundation and hopelessly relative.

There are several responses I can make, as a defender of religion of nature, to these assertions. The first response is that the trouble with reliance upon revelation as a source of ultimate truth and value is that there are *many different* supposed revelations, each with its own distinctive view of these matters—views that often do not agree with one another. How can we tell which one is entitled to our complete confidence and trust? It is not enough to have been reared in a culture where the authority of a particular revelation is assumed. We might have a strong inclination to rely upon that supposed revelation, in contrast with other claimants to revelation. But an inclination to believe something is not the same thing as being justified in believing something. Moreover, it is up to us humans to interpret and apply the meaning of any given putative revelation. History shows that there can be notorious and far-reaching differences in this regard.

And yet, without human interpretation and application of an alleged revelation, it can have little importance or meaning for human life. In addition, how can we tell with absolute certainty how much or how little the hand of human construction, imagination, and interpretation has played in the development of any putative revelation in its present form?[8] So we are not saved from the limitations and constraints of our finite humanity when we make appeal to the assumed revelations of an infinite being. There is no absolute guarantee of the reliability of claims to final wisdom in matters of faith and morals, no matter how sincerely and deeply these claims are thought to be based in the outlook of such a being. We should also note that the perspectivist metaphysics I laid out in chapter 4 gives reasons for denying the possibility of a completely comprehensive, all-knowing perspective on the world, even for God. No matter how inclusive and wide-ranging God's perspective might be thought to be, it is one perspective among many others and cannot be completely congruent with any one or all of those others.

The line of nihilist argument we are dealing with here also assumes a much-debated *correspondence theory* of truth and value. Claims to truth and value are said to be validated by the extent to which they correspond to or approximate to the mind of an infinite being and the exhaustive knowledge it has of the world. But not only is such exhaustive knowledge called into question by a perspectivist metaphysics, we can also dispute the model of warranted assertions of truth and value it assumes. How could we ever know that a claim to knowledge or value corresponds to the mind of an infinite being or to its vision of the world? How could we even know with certainty that it corresponds to any part of a supposedly objective world existing in serene detachment from fallible interpretations or points of view? I argued earlier that there is no such thing as an in-itself world—only a world (or, more properly worlds) constituted by the multiple standpoints and interrelations of perspectives. The best we can do in the way of attaining dependable knowledge, therefore, is to rely upon commonly accepted criteria of truth and value such as consistency and coherence; adequacy to relevant kinds of experience; cogency of logical argument; simplicity; fruitfulness in practice and in providing further insight or further paths of relevant inquiry; and the like. Once these criteria have been satisfied and continue to be satisfied, there is no further work we can do or need to do.

The issue of correspondence or approximation to something beyond the reach of these criteria should not trouble us. All searches for truth and value are the work of human beings with their finite means of investigation and testing. There is no pressing need—and no clearly definable or defensible way—for us to rely upon supernatural sources of knowledge, wisdom, or understanding. The outcomes of careful inquiry into matters of faith and morals may not yield absolute certainty or assurance, but they would seem to be far more reliable than outcomes of careless inquiry or of uncritical, unthinking submission to some allegedly infallible external authority. There is a wide middle ground between the absolute and the absurd. The nihilist argument now under consideration fails to recognize the importance and value of this capacious middle ground. Hopeless ignorance is not the sole alternative to absolute knowledge, even when the most critical matters of faith and morals are at stake.

We can conclude this section, then, by affirming on the basis of the arguments and reasons given above that the importance, value, and meaning of finite human life and of finite existence as such do not require that there be infinites or absolutes from which finite things derive or upon which they depend. Religion of nature asserts the sufficiency of the finite and rejoices in the abundant resources and goods nature provides for the living of our lives. Its affirmation is tempered, however, by acknowledgment of the menacing shadow of evil that haunts finite existence. Finitude and vulnerability go necessarily together: vulnerability to natural calamities, dangers, and accidents and to dark, perverse, and destructive inclinations and actions of human beings. How well does religion of nature equip us to deal with these two sorts of vulnerability? Responding to this question is the concern of the next section.

FINITE LIFE AND EVIL

Evil comes in many guises. The two most basic categories of such evils, as we have seen, are systemic natural evils and moral evils. Some evils in each of these two categories are at least partially preventable; others are not. Consider first systemic natural evils. We can show enough respect for nature as not deliberately to produce, or allow to be produced, conditions in it that make us or other creatures more susceptible to natural disasters. For example, we can avoid, as far as possible, pollution of the earth, seas and watercourses, and the atmosphere. We can avoid building our houses, schools, factories, and businesses in wetlands, on floodplains, or directly on seacoasts. We can stop laying waste to our rain forests. We can fight against erosion and the depletion of topsoil. We can drive cars that consume less gasoline and are low on pollution. And we can support government programs that encourage the production of these cars. We can develop or expand public transportation systems. We can utilize renewable sources of energy and ones that are less likely to pollute the atmosphere. We can recycle. We can endeavor to keep our human population under control. We can develop better ways of predicting and protecting ourselves against such things as earthquakes, tornadoes, and hurricanes.

We can take advantage of the techniques of preventive medicine to fend off debilitation and disease. We can avoid addictions and practices—smoking, drug use, bad diet, overeating, lack of exercise, stressful situations, etc.—that threaten our health. We can help the poor, the hungry, the sick, and the needy in our own neighborhoods and around the world. We can seek legislation against the abuses of factory farming. And we can work to protect endangered and other living species in whatever ways we can. These and similar tactics can help to protect against destructive potentialities of nature that threaten us and all forms of life.

But of course, no such tactics, no matter how elaborate or thorough, can protect us totally against systemic natural evils. We are finite beings and we live in a precarious world. If we are to live realistically within the world, we must take these two brute facts fully into account. Religion of nature helps to prepare us for life in this world by reminding us that we are not in complete control of things, that natural disasters are going to take place, that we must live with caution and care, that smaller scale accidents take place all around us and might at any moment impact our own lives or the lives of those we love, and that, as human beings, we are but a small part of an incredibly vast and intricate system that does not center on us and that combines predictable causal laws with imponderable workings of chance.

This system is ambiguous, as we have often had occasion to note, in that its many goods are made possible only when accompanied by many potential evils. For religion of nature, no quality or amount of petitionary prayer can alter these facts or be expected to weight the system's ambiguities in favor of those who pray. Nevertheless, religion of nature teaches us to reverence the system as a whole and to celebrate its essential rightness. We can give thanks for the gift of life and the goods nature bestows upon us and other creatures, and we humans can seek by our thought and action to be blessings to nature rather than blights upon it.

It is one thing to understand these matters intellectually. It is something quite different to put into effective practice the ones of them that are under our control and especially to come to terms in the depths of our emotional and existential being with those that are not. Both require a high quality of resourcefulness, dedication, and commitment. And these, in their turn, can be greatly strengthened by various types of spiritual practice such as regular meditation; repentance for past failures and weak resolve; aspiring in one's heart to do good and to find ways to do so effectively; giving fervent thanks for all the good things of the world; preparing oneself to be open and responsive to events of grace; searching for strength in oneself and in fellowship with others for encounters with systemic natural and moral evils; reaching out to help others—especially humans and nonhuman creatures most in need of our assistance and concern—and thereby focusing less intently upon oneself and one's own needs and desires; finding instruction and inspiration in the lives and teachings of exemplary moral and religious persons; and participating actively in the collective rituals, traditions, teachings, stories, songs, and work of religious communities that are sympathetic with, supportive of, or at least not inimical to the outlook of religion of nature.

Also highly relevant in this regard are taking time to explore and enjoy the abundant beauties of nature, to learn about and contemplate the intricate details of its operations, and to study and admire its distinctive life forms and their complex interrelations—interrelations that include us and our human communities. Above all, each of us humans can meditate regularly upon what it means to be a creature of nature, bone of its bone and flesh of its flesh. Strolling, hiking, camping, swimming, and other kinds of outdoor activity can greatly aid this process of meditation. The slanting rays of the sun through the trees seen while walking in a crisp autumn late afternoon, or the sight of a squadron of pelicans winging its way just above the waves of the blue-green Gulf of Mexico while one is bobbing in those same waves, can inspire and rejuvenate the soul. So too can the exhilaration of a steep mountain climb, with the panorama of meadows gleaming in the sun or curtained with clouds far below, and the distant summit beckoning above. There are dangers about, to be sure, but there are also feelings of restfulness and peace, and of sharing with other creatures the glories of nature. We can also contemplate the wonders of nature by reflecting on the powers nature has conferred upon us humans, powers made manifest in our cultures, languages, and technological achievements. We can do so in the home or on city streets, by attending a concert or reading a book, in school or at a political meeting, at work or at play, and not just by retreating to places of wilderness devoid of human habitation. By these and similar means we can deepen our sense of being at home in nature, of being sustained and renewed by its wonders, and of having profound responsibility to contribute to and not detract from its integrity and well-being.

But what if disaster strikes? What if we ourselves or someone close to us is hurt or killed? What if an accident causes sudden and severe disruption, tragedy, and pain? What if a life-threatening illness becomes unexpectedly manifest in a beloved person thought to be in sound good health? And what about those who are born with or are later afflicted with severe physical or mental disabilities and must suffer with them throughout their lives? If we have a grain of compassion and sympathy, are we not more apt to deplore than to celebrate the ways of nature in these and other similar sad circumstances? Bolstered by the vision of religion of nature, we can deeply regret such events but need not deplore or condemn the nature that produces them. There is no God to be blamed for them. They are not acts of forgetfulness, vengeance, or cruelty. They are ways of nature that affect us just as they affect all other living beings. They are part of the ambiguity of nature. None of us is immune to the dark side of this ambiguity, and it will eventually bring about our own deaths, the deaths of all those we love, and the final dissolution of all we have striven to accomplish.

Since we cannot escape being subject to the ambiguity of nature, our task is to find the courage to live in the face of it. Our task is to find the strength to affirm our own finitude and the finitude of everything around us. And our task is to support and help one another in times of sorrow and grief. Sometimes, this can best be done by our silent presence or by simple symbolic deeds, not by words. When I was a student in the Princeton Theological Seminary many years ago, I sat in a class being taught by the greatly loved and respected professor of Christian ethics, Paul Lehmann, who is now deceased. We were talking about how a minister should behave when visiting a person with a terminal illness who knows that his or her illness is terminal. "Perhaps the best thing you can do," he counseled, "is to fix that person a cup of tea." He did not mean this literally, I think, but what he meant was that a gesture of kindness and support sometimes means far more than even the most eloquent words, words that in any event are seldom adequate to the situation. We cannot resolve the ambiguities of nature by analyzing them away, and it is futile to try to do so, with ourselves or with others. But we can be fellow sufferers who understand, because we are all in the same boat. We cannot have the joys of nature or of our lives as natural beings without also expecting to experience their sorrows. Readiness for the one requires readiness for the other.

Religion of nature is honest and realistic in this regard. It offers us no pap, no panaceas, no empty promises. It does not build castles in the air. Instead, it brings us plumping down to earth. It says, "Find your courage, strength, and meaning here. You are a child of the earth, and there is no other place to go." This is the beginning and the end of religion of nature's wisdom. Is it enough? Perhaps it is not for some, but I find it to be sufficient. Religion of nature's realism about the intermingling light and darkness of the ways of nature girds my loins and refreshes my soul. For me, honesty is one of the central religious virtues, and I regard religion of nature as an entirely honest religious vision of how we ought to aspire to think, feel, and live as human beings. Its path is not easy, and sometimes it can be incredibly hard. This point helps to commend it as the appropriate path to follow in a world whose challenges, delights, and marvels are only made possible by the ever-present threat of its pitfalls, pains, and sorrows. To be is to be finite. And to be finite is, as I remarked earlier, to be vulnerable. This statement pertains to our world and everything in it, including ourselves. To live authentically as religious persons, we cannot hide this fact in a corner or pretend to find ways to evade it or make ourselves impervious to it. There is a fundamental distinction between genuine religion and bogus manipulative magic. But we can seek ways to build courage and strength in solitude and with one another for our inevitable encounters with nature's perils.

Sometimes terrible suffering can be accompanied by new opportunities to learn more deeply the lessons of sympathy and love. I heard recently about a mother who lost her beloved daughter to acute pneumonia when the daughter was in her early forties. The daughter had not been able to have children. Soon after the daughter's death, the mother offered to take care of her granddaughter's month-old son so that the granddaughter could work during the day. She later said that she would never have been able to cope with the tragic death of her daughter had she not been willing to undertake, on behalf of her granddaughter, the daily care of her baby. Helping two other persons in need enabled her to divert attention from her own suffering. Her experience with the baby also illustrated the important lesson that the chapter about tragic deaths is not the whole story of the universe; there is also the chapter about precious new life.

Let us shift our attention now from systemic natural evils to moral evils. Even though moral evils are generally under human control and therefore in principle avoidable or preventable, we have seen that there are situations where, in order to produce one kind of good or prevent one kind of evil, we have to commit or allow another kind of evil to take place. The best we can do in some circumstances is to choose between the lesser of two evils or to choose a good that can be obtained only at the price of the commission or allowance of an evil or of the sacrifice of a lesser good. Moral situations, in other words, are sometimes laden with in-principle ambiguity. There are such things as irreconcilable conflicts of goods or necessary choices between evils. In addition, moral evils deliberately committed or allowed by one person, group of persons, or institution may afflict another person, group, or institution in ways that are beyond the latter's prevention or control. The good of freedom contains the potentiality of evil abuses of that freedom, and the innocent can suffer greatly and with no recourse as a consequence of those abuses.

We can think of the widespread suffering of the Chinese at the hands of the Japanese during the 1930s and 1940s, recounted earlier, or we can recall the Killing Fields of Cambodia during the mid-1970s, in which an estimated two million Cambodians (or about 30 percent of the entire Cambodian population) died by starvation, torture, or execution as the result of malicious government policies. Closer to home and to our own time, we can think of reports in the daily newspapers of innocent victims of such criminal acts as murder, rape, theft, extortion, graft, terrorism, and genocide, and of those who are suffering horrendous effects of the unbridled violence of current wars and had no hand in bringing about those wars. We can also think of those who are routinely discriminated against and denied equal opportunities in society because of their skin colors, ethnic backgrounds, genders, sexual orientations, or ages. Then there are the victims of savage violence, sexual abuse, or criminal neglect in the home. Not all moral evils are of one's own doing; one can experience dire consequences of the evils brought about or allowed to occur by others. This is one aspect of the ambiguity of nature as reflected in the choices and actions of human beings or in the absence of their appropriate moral attention and concern.

The consequences and dangers of moral evil lie about us everywhere and every day. This is much more the case in some parts of the world than it is in the United States, and it is more so in some parts of the United

States than in others. But no area of the world is immune to the devasta-tions of moral evil. And none of us is guiltless, although some are guiltier than others. Every time we get into a car to drive to work or to the store, we take the risk of being maimed or killed by someone who is drunk, ir-responsible, or reckless in his or her driving. When we walk down a city street we are in danger of being mugged. There are people around who are ready to cheat us or take unfair advantage of us. Our governments sometimes cut corners, lie, tell half-truths, cover up miscalculations and mistakes, and commit themselves uncritically to foolish ideologies and ruinous policies. Our government representatives sometimes engage in shady practices in order to benefit financially from their positions of power or to ensure their reelections. And our businesses sometimes cook their books to avoid prosecu-tion, to gain illicit tax advantages, or to maximize their profits. Businesses are also sometimes ruthless in their attempts to gain an edge over their competitors, and they are sometimes guilty of cruel exploitation of their workers. In our unstable times, terrorism is a constant threat and can erupt anywhere in the world.

We ourselves are constantly tempted to compromise or ignore moral principles for the sake of some imagined benefit or gain, to give vent to our passions, or to avoid expending the time and effort required for us to address forthrightly important moral issues over which we can have some control. Moral evil is not only outside us but within us. Regular disdainful misuses of one's freedom can produce encrustations of habit that over time severely damage the quality and integrity of one's life. One can even become despicable to oneself and lose all confidence in one's ability to reform and become a better person. Hopeless, spiritless moral self-condemnation can result. And it can have devastating consequences for one's obligations to and relations with others.

Of course, hopelessness and brokenness of spirit rarely stem solely from simple cumulative misuses of personal freedom; their causes are generally more complex and can be physiological as well as sociological in character. In any event, this condition cries out for compassion, forgiveness, patience, and assistance on the part of those not so afflicted and those most competent to help. A crucial part of this help is enabling the afflicted individual to gain a new sense of personal dignity, responsibility, and freedom.

There is no automatic solution to these and other problems of moral evil. In religion of nature, there is no God to bail us out, clean up after us, forgive us, or empower us. And there is no use trying to minimize the cor-rosive effects of moral evils on one's own character and behavior; on one's loved ones, friends, neighbors, and community; on the course of civilization; and on the natural environment. Some forms of moral evil require the at-tention of medical doctors and psychological counselors. They also stand in need of fundamental improvements in our penal systems, with much more emphasis on and resources directed to rehabilitation than mere punishment.

The moral dimensions of education are of critical importance, as are the character and example of role models in society as a whole and the powerful influences of the communications media. Moral evil is here to stay, by all indications, and we must learn how to be more effective in our battles against it and in learning how best to live in the face of it.

The sources of our greatest hope in this battle, I believe, are the capacity for and impulse toward goodness that lie within each of us. This does not necessarily mean that we are fundamentally good by nature, but what it does mean is that we have a powerful *potential* to be good if we can learn to act in accordance with our deep—if sometimes only potential and relatively undeveloped—sense of moral obligation, responsibility, and opportunity. It is important to reflect upon the fact that there is an abundance of moral goodness in the world that runs counter to a threatening despair about the large amount of moral evil it also contains. There are stalwart exemplars of the moral life in history and in the present who can help to light the way. Each one of us can no doubt think of people of this sort whom one knows personally or who live in one's own community.[9]

Not only is there a tendency toward evil in the human heart, there is also a marked tendency toward decency, goodness, and high moral aspiration and action. Were this not so, it is doubtful that we could have survived as a species. The possibility of enduring social order is predicated upon the capacity of humans to live together in relative harmony and peace. The deep-rootedness of that capacity is no less evident, and I think much more conspicuously evident, than is our human capacity for cruelty, strife, and disruption. There is a mystery of the extent of moral goodness as well as a mystery of the extent of moral evil in human life. But the former mystery is generally not sufficiently attended to or discussed.

Why is there so much moral goodness in the world? Just to ask this question is to remind ourselves not only of how mysterious but also of how reassuring this familiar fact is. Amicable behavior among most of us most of the time is the general rule, and it provides the rarely noticed background for breaches of moral principles that are newsworthy precisely because of their striking contrast with this background and that therefore get actively reported in the media. We need also to remind ourselves that impressive moral strides have been made in certain periods of human history alongside its continuing moral evils. The abolition of slavery, child labor laws, legislation against racial segregation, laws guaranteeing women the right to vote, the establishment of the United Nations, and government assistance for the poor and for the disabled are salient examples in the West and other parts of the world.

Religious faith, including a religion of nature, can motivate, encourage, and inspire us to build upon this capacity for and tendency toward moral goodness in ourselves and to work together for their actualization and incorporation into our institutions and societies. The right kinds of legislation and education can contribute mightily toward this end, as can the moral rearing of our children and our careful, discerning choice of political leaders. The power of personal example should never be underestimated. There is no guarantee of the triumph of moral goodness over moral evil, but there is substantial hope for its progress against the fortresses of evil. Our concerted choices and actions can help to make that hope more confident and secure. With freedom comes responsibility, and with responsibility comes the possibility of making a significant positive difference in what is accomplished and how things turn out. This is the bright side of the moral ambiguity that is made manifest and inevitable by our possession of personal freedom. As my wife Pamela Crosby puts the matter, "We humans can be sources as well as beneficiaries of the numerous forces for good at work in the world. The power and effectiveness of those forces is to some appreciable degree dependent upon us, not on a supernatural being."

So we must help one another, rely upon one another, and appeal to one another for insight and strength. In addition we must learn how to open ourselves to the healing powers of the nonhuman parts of nature, to the larger community of natural beings and their environments of which we are an integral part. It is a community that brought us into being and sustains us in being. It existed before each of us and will continue to exist after us, supporting and sustaining those who outlive us, including our children and their children. We can contribute in important ways to its well-being even as it contributes to our own. We can draw upon its restorative powers and be humbled and inspired by its vastness and splendor. We can experience deeper, more lasting community with our fellow humans even as we join together in learning how to be more responsible and receptive citizens of the whole community of earth.

Religious faith can not only inspire and motivate us to live more purposeful, caring, productive, and contributing lives within ourselves and in community with others—including in these times, one hopes, with our nonhuman others. It can also contribute fundamentally to our sense of orientation and direction in the world, to our ability to navigate among its shoals and dangers with a clear awareness of where we need to go and what goals we need to steer toward. All religions do this by supplying us with a kind of chart or map that orients us in the course of our lives as human beings on this earth and in the context of the cosmos as a whole.[10] I have tried in this book to unfold the map of religion of nature, to spread it out on the table and describe its features in some detail, to compare and contrast it with certain other maps, and to recommend it to my readers as a dependable guide for our religious lives and for all the other parts of our lives that critically depend upon a realistic and sustaining religious vision.

NOTES

CHAPTER 1. RELIGION OF NATURE
AS A FORM OF RELIGIOUS NATURALISM

1. I use the male pronoun in talking about God, partly to avoid the awkwardness of "he/she" and similar locutions, but more fundamentally because this has been the traditional way of speaking of God, and I am referring for the most part to traditional notions of God. When I speak of more recent notions of God, such as that of process theology, I will continue to use male pronouns for the sake of consistency. However, readers should be reminded that this usage is controversial, and rightly so. A problem connected with the idea of God is the heavy overtones of patriarchy and male chauvinism that have resounded throughout historical expressions of the idea.

2. I employed this image in an earlier work; see D. A. Crosby 1997: 357.

3. Isaiah 45:7, in *The Holy Scriptures According to the Masoretic Text* (Philadelphia: The Jewish Publication Society of America, 1952).

4. Some parts of this chapter are loosely based on D. A. Crosby 2003a.

CHAPTER 2. AMBIGUITIES OF NATURE

1. For this description of the influenza pandemic I drew upon the essay "The Spanish Flu" in the online encyclopedia *Wikipedia*. HTTP:<http://www.en.wikipedia. org/wiki/Spanishflu.html> (accessed 14 September 2005) and another essay entitled "The Influenza Pandemic of 1918" by Molly Billings, modified RDS 2005. HTTP: <http://www. Stanford.edu/group/virus/uda. html> (accessed 14 September 2005). A definitive treatment of the pandemic is Alfred W. Crosby 1990.

2. My information on the December 2004 earthquake and tsunami is derived from two sources: "2004 Indian Ocean Earthquake" in *Wikipedia*. HTTP: http:// en.wikipedia.org/wiki/Tsunami.html> (accessed 15 September 2005) and the BBC news feature "Tsunami: Anatomy of a Disaster" by Helen Lambourne. HTTP: <http://news. bbc.co.uk/1/hi/in_depth/world/2004. html> (accessed 15 September 2005).

3. This account of Japanese atrocities is based for the most part on Bradley 2004, but with additional support from the following sources: Utsumi Aiko, "Japan's World War II Policy: Indifference and Irresponsibility." HTTP: <http://japanfocus. org/article.asp?id=276. html> (accessed 20 September 2005); Ralph Blumenthal, "Japan's World War II Atrocities: Comparing the Unspeakable to the Unthinkable," *New York Times*, March 7, 1999. HTTP: <http//: www2.gol.com/users/coynerhm/ japan_WWII_atrocities.html> (accessed 20 September 2005); "Forgotten Holocaust,"

an interview by David Gergen on February 26, 1998, with Iris Chang, author of *The Rape of Nanking: The Forgotten Holocaust of World War II.* PBS Online News Hour. HTTP: <http://www.pbs.org/newshour/gergen/february98/chang_2-20.html> (accessed 20 September 2005). The examples of the Sand Creek Massacre and the American war against the Philippine freedom fighters were also used by Bradley to make the point that Americans are far from being guiltless when it comes to atrocities (see Bradley 2004: 10–11, 67–71). An extensive account of the atrocities of Japanese soldiers in the city of Nanking is contained in the above-mentioned book by Iris Chang (See Chang 1997). Some historians have questioned the factual accuracy and evidential support of Chang's book at certain points. See, for example, the reviews of Chang's book by Timothy M. Kelly and Robert Entenmann HTTP: <http://www.edogawa-u.ac.jp/~tmkelly/research_review_nanking.html> (accessed 7 September, 2006); HTTP: <http://www.hartford-hwp.com/archives/55/481.html> (accessed 7 September, 2006).

4. For other glaring examples of moral evil, see the six discussed and analyzed in Kekes 2005 and the psychoanalytic study of Adolf Hitler's "malignant aggression" in chapter 13 of Fromm 1973.

5. Parts of this chapter are loosely based on D. A. Crosby 2005b.

CHAPTER 3. NATURE AS THE FOCUS OF RELIGIOUS FAITH

1. For a discussion of Alfred North Whitehead's views on the nature of religion, see D. A. Crosby 1983.

2. D. A. Crosby 2002 is also devoted to a defense of religion of nature as a type of religious faith. See especially part 3 of that book.

CHAPTER 4. PERSPECTIVISM, PLURALISM, AND AMBIGUITY

1. I thank Tyron Inbody (in a written communication) for bringing to my attention the possibly misleading character of my regular use of the singular term *nature*, a use that might—if not clarified—suggest a similarity to monotheism in the idea of nature as religiously ultimate. Instead of routinely regarding nature as one or as "it," we should remind ourselves at least on occasion to think of nature as many or as "they." Traditional notions of divine simplicity and unity, to say nothing of immutability, do not carry over into nature as I conceive it.

2. For a clear and perceptive presentation of some central ideas of Advaita Vedanta Hinduism see Deutsch 1973, especially chapters 1 through 4.

3. The first section of this chapter contains some themes of my article "Two Perspectives on Metaphysical Perspectivism: Nietzsche and Whitehead" (D. A. Crosby 2007). This article can be consulted for information on a perspectivist metaphysics as Friedrich Nietzsche and Alfred North Whitehead conceive it and for critical comments on their respective views. See especially the last two sections of this article for an analysis of interrelations between perspectivism and pluralism and a brief defense of the perspectivist-pluralist position.

CHAPTER 5. RELIGIOUS RIGHTNESS AND MORAL VALUE

1. We should not fail to note that Gautama's enlightenment was made possible, in part, by his act of abandoning his home and family: an illustration of the intentional sacrifice of a moral good for the sake of a religious good and also of the sometimes highly ambiguous relations between good and evil in general.

CHAPTER 6. COPING WITH AMBIGUITY

1. Quoted in the *Yukon News* and reprinted in *The Week* magazine, May 5, 2006: 17.

2. For a detailed discussion of the philosophy of nihilism, of a number of debatable assumptions upon which it rests, and of lessons we can learn from it, see D. A. Crosby 1988. I show in this book, for example, that traditional Christian theists such as the Russian novelist Fyodor Dostoevsky and the German Roman Catholic theologian Hans Küng defend their theism on the basis of assumptions such as the ones I describe in this section, while the French Existentialists Albert Camus and Jean Paul Sartre conclude from surprisingly similar kinds of assumption that human life is absurd. The Jewish theologian Martin Buber contends that ethics collapses into a hopeless, destructive relativism without a personal relation to God as the Absolute. He writes, "Only out of a personal relationship with the Absolute can the absoluteness of the ethical co-ordinates arise without which there is no complete awareness of self." And he states that "always it is the religious which bestows, the ethical which receives." By "the religious" he means a reciprocal, I-Thou relation between humans and God as the Absolute (Buber 1988: 98; see also chs. 6 and 7 *passim*).

3. An explication of processes, principles, and theories that can be drawn upon to account for the evolutionary emergence of life from nonlife and of humans from earlier forms of life is contained in chapters 5 and 6 of D. A. Crosby 2005a. I argue in this book for an evolutionary account that is not reductionist but emergentist because genuinely new and irreducible kinds of possibility and actuality come into being with increasing complexity of biological organization.

4. Leibniz did not allow for ultimate chance or contingency in the universe. He argued that everything in it occurs as ordained and caused by God in order that this universe can be the best of all possible worlds. See Leibniz 1951: 92–96 for some of his statements of and arguments for the idea of sufficient reason.

5. In D. A. Crosby 2005a, I defend the idea that chance is as fundamental a concept as is the concept of efficient causality for interpreting the nature of reality. Interworkings of causality and chance are crucial for an adequate understanding of time and possibility, the development of the present cosmos, the emergence of life from nonlife, the emergence of human beings, and the development of consciousness and freedom.

6. I argue at length for this conclusion in chapter 5 of D. A. Crosby 2002.

7. The Book of Job in the Hebrew Bible can be interpreted as calling into serious question the absolute moral goodness of God, at least in any sense that humans

are competent to understand. In this interpretation, the God of Job is analogous to nature as I interpret and understand it. Both are highly ambiguous from a moral standpoint and yet both are viewed as richly deserving of religious reverence and devotion. In the parlance of the present book, God is religiously "right" in Job's eyes, and unqualifiedly so, although Job's God is initially experienced as morally ambiguous and remains so throughout the book. The book of Job also calls into question the "virtue-prosperity" equation of the Deuteronomic interpretation of Israel's religious history, namely, the conviction that strict obedience to God will ensure prosperity and well-being for the Jewish people, while disobedience will bring divine punishment and deserved affliction. The book of Job does not offer any kind of theodicy; it lays stark emphasis on the *problem* of theodicy—or perhaps even upon the utter uselessness of trying to solve the problem conceptually. This general line of thought was suggested to me in written correspondence by J. Thomas Howe, although he should not be held accountable for the specific way I develop it in this note. His suggestion is an excellent one, and I am grateful to him for it.

8. Ehrman 2005 is a thorough, engaging discussion of this problem as it relates to the origins of the Christian New Testament and the omissions, additions, and variant readings in its extant early manuscripts.

9. In chapter 8 of D. A. Crosby 2002 I elaborate on the capacity for goodness in human beings and present several impressive examples of it. Readers should also recall the inspiring examples of my friends Norene Chase and Anne Rudloe, discussed in chapter 3.

10. I owe the metaphor of a map to Mary Midgley. See Midgley 1986: 49, 201.

WORKS CITED

Anselm. 1948. *Prosologium*. Translated by Sidney Norton Deane. La Salle, IL: Open Court.

Aquinas, T. 1948. *Introduction to Saint Thomas Aquinas*. Edited by Anton C. Pegis. New York: The Modern Library.

Bradley, J. 2004. *Flyboys: A true story of courage*. New York and Boston: Little, Brown. Back Bay Books.

Buber, M. 1988. *Eclipse of God: Studies in the relation between religion and philosophy*. Introduction by Robert M. Seltzer. Amherst, NY: Humanity Books.

Chang, I. 1997. *The rape of Nanking: The forgotten holocaust of World War II*. New York: Basic Books.

Conze, E. 1959. *Buddhism: Its essence and development*. Harper Torchbooks.

Cook, F. H. 1989. The jewel net of Indra. In *Nature in Asian traditions of thought*, ed. J. Baird Callicott and Roger T. Ames. Albany: State University of New York Press, 213–29.

Crosby, A. W. 1990. *America's forgotten pandemic: The influenza of 1918*. Cambridge: Cambridge University Press.

Crosby, D. A. 1981. *Interpretive theories of religion*. The Hague: Mouton.

———. 1983. Religion and solitariness. In *Explorations in Whitehead's philosophy*, ed. Lewis S. Ford and George L. Kline. New York: Fordham University Press, 149–69.

———. 1988. *The specter of the absurd: Sources and criticisms of modern nihilism*. Albany: State University of New York Press.

———. 1997. Finite is all right! Confessions of a slow learner. In *Pragmatism, neo-pragmatism, and religion: Conversations with Richard Rorty*, ed. Charley D. Hardwick and Donald A. Crosby. New York: Peter Lang, 357–82.

———. 2002. *A religion of nature*. Albany: State University of New York Press.

———. 2003a. Naturism as a form of religious naturalism. *Zygon: Journal of Religion and Science* 38, no. 1 (March): 117–20.

———. 2003b. Transcendence and immanence in a religion of nature. *American Journal of Theology and Philosophy* 24, no. 3 (September): 245–59.

———. 2005a. *Novelty*. Lanham, MD: Lexington Books.

———. 2005b. The distinctiveness of religion and religious value. *American Journal of Theology and Philosophy* 26, no. 3 (September): 199–206.

———. 2007. Two perspectives on metaphysical perspectivism: Nietzsche and Whitehead. *The Pluralist* 2, no. 3 (Fall): 57–76.

Cusanus, N. 1954. *Of learned ignorance*. Translated by Germain Heron. London: Routledge and Kegan Paul.

Deutsch, E. 1973. *Advaita Vedanta: A philosophical reconstruction*. Honolulu: The University Press of Hawaii.

Dixon, W. McN. 1937. *The human situation*. New York: Longmans, Green.

Dupré, J. 2003. *Darwin's legacy: What evolution means today*. Oxford: Oxford University Press.

Ehrman, B. D. 2005. *Misquoting Jesus: The story behind who changed the Bible and why*. New York: HarperCollins.

Fromm, E. 1973. *The anatomy of human destructiveness*. New York: Henry Holt. An Owl Book.

Hare, R. M. 1973. The simple believer. In *Religion and morality*, ed. Gene Outka and John P. Reeder Jr. Garden City: Anchor Press/Doubleday. Anchor Books, 393–427.

Hick, J. 1966. *Evil and the god of love*. London: Macmillan.

———. 1990. *Philosophy of religion*. Fourth Edition. Englewood Cliffs, NJ: Prentice-Hall.

Inbody, T. L. 1997. *The transforming god: An interpretation of suffering and evil*. Louisville: Westminster John Knox Press.

James, W. 1962. Author's preface to the will to believe and other essays. In *Essays on Faith and Morals*, selected by Ralph Barton Perry. Cleveland and New York: World. Meridian Books.

Kekes, J. 2005. *The roots of evil*. Ithaca: Cornell University Press.

Leibniz, G. W. F. von. 1951. Excerpts from various documents in *Leibniz selections*, ed. Philip P. Wiener. New York: Scribner's.

Loomer, B. 1987. The size of God. In *The size of God: The theology of Bernard Loomer in context*, ed. William Dean and Larry E. Axel. Macon, GA: Mercer University Press.

Midgley, M. 1986. *Wickedness: A philosophical essay*. London: Ark Paperbacks.

Mill, J. S. 1967. *Utilitarianism*. Indianapolis: Bobbs-Merrill. The Library of Liberal Arts.

Nietzsche, F. 1968. *The will to power*. Edited by Walter Kaufmann. Translated by R. J. Hollingdale and Walter Kaufmann. New York: Vintage Books.

Peat, F. D. 1997. *Infinite potential: The life and times of David Bohm*. Reading, MA: Addison-Wesley. Helix Books.

Phipps, R. P. 2005. A Whiteheadian theory of creative, synthetic learning and its relevance to educational reform in China. In *Alfred North Whitehead on learning and education: Theory and application*, ed. Franz G. Riffert. Newcastle: Cambridge Scholars Press, 159–98.

Power, W. L. 1997. Imago Dei—Imitatio Dei. *International Journal for Philosophy of Religion* 42: 131–41.

Rawlings, M. K. 1942. *Cross Creek*. New York: Grosset and Dunlap.

Reese, W. L. 1980. *Dictionary of philosophy and religion: Eastern and Western thought*. Atlantic Highlands, NJ: Humanities Press.

Rollin, B. E. 2006. *Science and ethics*. New York: Cambridge University Press.

Rudloe, A. 2002. *Butterflies on a sea wind: Beginning Zen*. Kansas City, KS: Andrews McMeel Publishing.

Shaw, M. 1995. *Nature's grace: Essays on H. N. Wieman's finite theism*. New York: Peter Lang.

Suzuki, D. T. 1971. *Zen and Japanese culture*. Bollingen Series, volume 64. Princeton: Princeton University Press.

Tu W.-M. 1989. The continuity of being: Chinese visions of nature. In *Nature in Asian traditions of thought: Essays in environmental philosophy*, ed. J. Baird Callicott and Roger T. Ames. Albany: State University of New York Press, 67–78.

Whitehead, A. N. 1929. *Religion in the making*. New York: Macmillan.

———. 1978. *Process and reality*. Corrected Edition, ed. David Ray Griffin and Donald W. Sherburne. New York: Free Press.

Wieman, H. N., and Walter M. H. 1938. *The growth of religion*. Chicago: Willett, Clark.

Wieman, H. N. 1946. *The source of human good*. Chicago: University of Chicago Press.

INDEX